VERMONT
perspectives

VERMONT
perspectives

SENSE OF PLACE, STATE OF MIND

ANNE AVERYT

Essex, Connecticut

Globe Pequot

An imprint of Globe Pequot, the trade division of
The Rowman & Littlefield Publishing Group, Inc.
4501 Forbes Blvd., Suite 200
Lanham, MD 20706
www.rowman.com

Distributed by NATIONAL BOOK NETWORK

Unless otherwise noted, these essays aired in earlier form as Commentaries on Vermont Public Radio. The Author wishes to thank Vermont Public Co. for permission to use these commentaries. The commentaries are available at https://www.vpr.org/people/anne-averyt.

British Library Cataloguing in Publication Information available

Library of Congress Cataloging-in-Publication Data

Names: Averyt, Anne, 1946– author.
Title: Vermont perspectives : sense of place, state of mind / Anne Averyt.
Description: Guilford, Connecticut : Globe Pequot, [2022] | Summary:
  "Author Anne Averyt explores with insight and humor the keen sense of
  place and solid footing in local values that shape Vermonters' views of
  home and the world beyond. A nine-year veteran commentator on Vermont
  Public Radio, Averyt shares her experience in this expanded collection
  of her essays"—Provided by publisher.
Identifiers: LCCN 2021062465 (print) | LCCN 2021062466 (ebook) | ISBN
  9781493066056 (paperback) | ISBN 9781493066063 (epub)
Subjects: LCSH: Averyt, Anne, 1946– | Vermont—Anecdotes.
Classification: LCC F49 .A84 2022 (print) | LCC F49 (ebook) | DDC
  974.3—dc23/eng/20220204
LC record available at https://lccn.loc.gov/2021062465
LC ebook record available at https://lccn.loc.gov/2021062466

♾️ The paper used in this publication meets the minimum requirements of American National Standard for Information Sciences—Permanence of Paper for Printed Library Materials, ANSI/NISO Z39.48-1992.

To my sons, Alan and Kevin, who have chosen a Vermont way of life.

ACKNOWLEDGMENTS

FROM DREAM TO REALITY IS A LONG AND WINDING ROAD. THIS COLLEC-
tion was born in the snowy winter of 2010 when my first radio commentary aired. Since then, many people have offered encouragement and
support.

Sarah Bartlett is the star in my night sky. A constant, encouraging
my dreams, sharpening my perceptions, honing my texts. She is mentor
and muse, but most of all, my friend, "phenomenally." Jeanne Cariati joins
Sarah as soul mate and stalwart literary sister, reading drafts, offering
insights, encouraging balance.

For sharing their love, their boundless curiosity and sheer joie de vivre,
I hug my granddaughters, Eliza, Lainey, and Marcella. Their sense of wonder opens my eyes to see and my heart to feel. Thanks to my sons, Kevin
and Alan, who from the sidelines offer counsel and reality checks; and to
my sibling clan, loyal and loving. Special thanks to Bill Averyt, longtime
friend and kindred spirit, who first lifted my eyes to see possibility.

Thanks to my editor and mentor, Betty Smith, producer of the Commentary Series on Vermont Public Radio, who taught me that you can
say a lot in a few words. And to Amy Lyons, editorial director at Globe
Pequot. Her vision and expertise brought this book to fruition.

Finally, to Tom and Nicole Chittenden, special thanks. They are the
proprietors of the "many acre garden" who opened their home and their
hearts to share Vermont with me. And to Robin Westen. When she first
read my manuscript, Robin encouraged me not just to dream a book, but
to go out and find a publisher!

An inspiring village . . .

Contents

*I love Vermont because of her hills and valleys,
her scenery and invigorating climate, but most of all
because of her indomitable people.*

—CALVIN COOLIDGE

A Vermonter eats apple pie for breakfast.

—RURAL SAYING

Ways of Seeing

I am a wordsmith, not a visual artist, but I share Paul Gauguin's palette principle. Like Gauguin, "I close my eyes in order to see." Perhaps a better way to say it is that I close my two eyes in order to see more clearly with my third eye, to be able to look through my mind's eye.

A third eye is a wonderful thing. A third-eye view of the world looks down from above and sees from below. It peeks out and it peers in. It sees what two eyes miss, and it misses what is not worth seeing. The third eye is the one through which visionaries see, and it is through the vision of the mind's eye that children dream their world. That rich and wonderful world children step into before they are admonished to stay within the lines, stand up straight, not get their hands dirty, or ever make a mess.

There are, of course, ways of seeing and ways of seeing. There is metaphorical seeing—complex "adult" pictures drawn with allegory, paradox, and inference—pictures meant to impress with the mind spin of intellect.

Children and those called "foolish" often see the world in a very different way. They delight in the fantasy of a world pictured literally. Have you ever stood and laughed with a child in a *downpour of cats and dogs*? Have you ever had the sheer pleasure of sailing in *a pea-green boat*, watched a *cow* leapfrog *over the moon* or chased a runaway *dish and spoon*?

Maybe Gauguin only closed his eyes because the tropical sun was too bright. Maybe he closed his eyes because a swarm of gnats was buzzing about his head. I like to believe he closed his eyes because he was a seer, because he believed you see more with three eyes than with two. That he understood how little distortion there is when we look through the lens of imagination, when we see with wonder, when we open wide our hearts to dream.

—Anne Averyt, 2022

SEASONAL TASTINGS

HOME IS WHERE ...

SCIENTISTS HAVE NOW MAPPED EIGHT THOUSAND GALAXIES TRYING TO figure out where in the world—or more precisely, where in the universe— we are. They want to know where on the celestial map Earth really resides—I guess that's important to know if you're out for a Sunday ride in the universe and you need to turn on your GPS to guide you home.

Finding home is a quest we all undertake at some point in our lives. In terms of our cosmic address, planet Earth resides in the Milky Way galaxy, which is part of a cluster of galaxies in a larger formation known as a supercluster. Thanks to the new data, researchers now know the Milky Way is floating on the outer edge of a previously unmapped supercluster they've named Laniakea, the Hawaiian word for "immeasurable heaven."

But long before scientists began searching for our place in space, we humans were trying to find our home here on Earth, and it's not always a physical location. Back in the first century AD the Roman observer, Pliny the Elder, said, "Home is where the heart is." And I think he meant that home is where we feel content, where we feel at peace, where we're happy.

Now, I wasn't born in Vermont, but for more than forty years I've called this Green Mountain state my home. It's the place I always want to come back to, no matter how far away I travel. And I'm not alone.

A recent study confirms that Vermonters are most content being Vermonters. We love our home state, and it's about more than just the spectacular scenery and clean air. Based on data compiled by Gallop Healthways research, Vermont comes in sixth in the nation in terms of well-being. Our life expectancy—eighty-plus years—is the fifth highest in the country, and our unemployment average is among the lowest. But it's our healthy lifestyle and low crime rate that really set our state apart.

Vermont is one of the safest states in the union, and when it comes to healthy living, Vermonters lead the nation. We eat more healthy foods, especially fresh vegetables and fruit. We exercise more regularly, and most of us report feeling physically healthy.

So, while scientists continue their quest to pinpoint Earth's exact location in the "immeasurable heaven" of the universe, here on Earth, we Vermonters already know our home address is in the Green Mountains. And it's more than just our physical location. It's where our hearts are.

MIDSUMMER MAJESTY

It's the first sign of fall, says my friend, farmer of the many acre garden—the Yellow Transparent. Four motley, misshapen apples sit sunning on his deck table. He's just picked them, and I marvel at a midsummer apple harvest. It's an old-brand apple, Tom tells me, one that ripens and passes so quickly it's easy to overlook. They aren't good for much, he adds, except applesauce and that first apple pie of the season.

Fresh apple pie in midsummer sounds pretty good to me, I tell him, and he says you need to make it while the early apples are still tart, not yet completely ripe. Tom's wife grew up on a farm in Northern Vermont, a stone's throw from Canada. She remembers picking all varieties of wild apples as a kid.

Because the trees weren't tended, the apples were often small and gnarled, pocked with brown spots that indicated possible worm inhabitants. You had to eat around the brown spots, Nicole recalled, "And before you swallowed, you'd better check to make sure you hadn't bitten into a worm or half of one. If you did, you just spit it out and kept on eating."

To me it sounded like a 1950s vignette straight out of the mega-movie *The Tree of Life*.

Summer is in full swing now all around the back deck at my friends', the proprietors of the many acre garden. Nestled under the eve of their upper deck is a soon-to-be vacated nest of baby robins, and by this weekend more vegetables will be ready for harvesting. "The end of store-bought produce is upon us," Tom announces with satisfaction.

We are sitting around the outside table, feasting on early chard and cucumbers, the first grilled zucchini of the summer, and fresh chives and dill sprinkled on our baked potatoes. The lanky green beans are ready for picking, and growing fat in brown earth are the onions, potatoes, and beets. Already the incredibly delicate asparagus is over; tall willowy stalks are the only remaining evidence of good eating.

The deck at the many acre plot looks east, and the rolling Greens sit in the distance, their presence a quiet statement. It's easier to paint summer in Vermont than to describe it—the colors are lush and the palette is verdant. Ireland may be called emerald, but I don't think anywhere else dances a green jig quite the way Vermont does.

Recently, I returned to Vermont after a brief foray into those concrete fields of hometown Philadelphia. As the plane eased through the clouds, seeming to ride on a gentle wind, the Green Mountains rolled and gently peaked, then sank deep into green, green valleys. Small lakes with irregular edges dotted the patchwork earth-quilt beneath me; and Camel's Hump sat majestic and sphinxlike, presiding over it all. Vermont in summer, welcoming me home.

ABUNDANT HARVEST

My friends of the many acre garden chose July to go on vacation. Early harvesttime. I thought it was early Christmas. They asked me to come pick their crops; and visions of zucchini and green beans, ruby beets, and leafy lettuce danced in my head.

But ten days into their two-week vacation, three long arduous harvesting expeditions behind me, I was humble and in awe of the produce farmer. And I couldn't wait for the absentee landlords to return.

I grew up in the concrete city of Philadelphia, and corn, cantaloupe, and tomatoes came fresh in summer from truck farms in Jersey. My mother bought "just enough vegetables" for dinner at Kim's Market in Fox Chase. There were no Fresh Air expeditions for city kids back then, so I never learned to tell a flowering weed from a green bean blossom.

I have learned a few things since then. After four decades in Vermont, I know those voluptuous yellow blooms guarded by spreading vines and umbrella leaves are not for picking, that one day they will break out of their chrysalis and become succulent squash.

I also know that chard, cilantro, and basil grow like morning glories. Here today, more tomorrow. I know there is a limit to the variety of ways one can cook chard—or kale; that even if I eat three salads a day, there's more lettuce left in the garden than I have neighbors.

Before they slipped away on vacation, my friends gave me the garden tour. Mr. Farmer pointed out the different species on his estate, but I can't read a road map, let alone navigate the twenty-odd crop groups in his four garden plots, all of them in basic green. We are talking serious gardening.

There are a gazillion tomato plants growing randomly around the many acre garden, but red never happened on my watch. I couldn't even find enough plump green tomatoes for a good old-fashioned Southern fry.

I did ferret out a few mini summer squashes, but the zucchini hid under a green leafy overhang. I harvested three overweight baby zucchini and left their Godzilla uncle to fatten for the Champlain Valley Fair. If it garners a blue ribbon, it's mine.

Many visions of revenge swirled in my head during those two weeks of travail. But I know, come Saturday afternoons throughout August and early into fall, my friends will share their bounty when I drop in to say hello. They'll have vegetables ripe and already picked.

This year's harvest taught me more lessons than just how to hunt for hidden vegetables. I now have a new appreciation for the hard work of abundance. Having walked the garden path, I will tip my sun hat to my friends and farmers everywhere, now that I know what it takes to produce produce.

SWAN SONG OF SUMMER

THE FREIGHT TRAIN OF FALL IS BARRELING DOWN THE TRACKS. THE scent of September is heavy in the air.

Somehow, I never seem to outgrow the school calendar. Summer officially starts for me in mid-June when schools shut their doors—even though more than half a century has passed since I walked out of Rowland Elementary and into the summer air of suburban Philadelphia.

In the same way, the rite of summer's passing is marked by an end of August aria and the crooning of September's song.

The cadence of the school calendar seems to set the pace for our entire lives. No matter what the Gregorian calendar says, summer only stretches from mid-June to early September. The holidays we look forward to are the memories of childhood freedom—Thanksgiving, Christmas, Presidents' Day, spring break. Time past carries us into time present, or as T. S. Eliot said, "Footfalls echo in memory—time future is contained in time past." At least, that's how it feels to me.

I still think of fall as it smelled to a teenager running the school hockey fields. I still hear the roar of the partisan hometown fans at the Friday-afternoon football game, and I still cruise in memory with my friends, riding through town, horns blaring, declaring victory.

Right now, in my backyard, the white wild roses are blooming, singing their swan song of summer. In the front yard, the fall hydrangeas are growing fat, infusing the air with their sweet scent as I approach the door. I know autumn's come. For schoolkids, fall carries the promise of a new year, while for me, in the autumn of my years, it is a wistful harbinger of snows soon to flurry and the approach of long months of house arrest, nestled in front of the woodstove of winter.

It is about anticipation—about looking forward, about the crisp air of change. Already, I've shifted my mental focus to fall chores. I'm cleaning up the garden and cleaning out the attic, filling my car trunk with old necessities earmarked for the autumn church yard sale.

My life moves forward along with the seasons. Although my children no longer wait at the corner for the school bus, and I no longer run the hockey field, the school bell still rings out in early September, reminding me—it's time to get dressed and ready for a new year.

REWRITING NOVEMBER

IT'S NOVEMBER, THAT QUIET TIME OF YEAR. THE LEAVES ARE GONE, color drained from the hillsides. In my yard, the maples' yellow leaves held on the longest, but now all that remains is the brown of the oaks. The willow is bent, as if weeping summer's loss.

I've always dreaded the encroaching darkness of November—the time of year that for me is most SAD. It triggers my seasonal affective disorder and sends me in search of my happy light, the 10,000 lux light box that offers synthetic sunshine on a cloudy day. Thank goodness for the light, because often I find it hard to be happy in November.

This is the cloudiest time of the year in Vermont. Burlington lags just behind Seattle with the least amount of annual sunlight. In November and December, the cold settles in and darkness gobbles up more and more of the daylight. My spirits dip, the world grows gray, and I feel blue.

But this year I'm trying to rewrite my autumn narrative. My granddaughters think of fall as a magical season. It's that wonderful time when leaves are transformed into towering mounds, inviting free falls. Likewise, Vermont hunters wait all year for the thrill of the chase in November and gather at early-morning breakfasts to swap stories. I too feel the seasonal excitement as signs begin to sprout up along roadsides announcing ski swaps, holiday bazaars, and chicken suppers.

If in late autumn, the leaves are gone, so too are the busloads of tourists and roads crowded with leaf peepers. We have Vermont mostly to ourselves during the seasonal segue from noisy autumn to the peaceful white of winter. It's a time of transition when we clear up the garden, stow the lawn furniture, and get ready for long months of hibernation.

It's the last chance to split and stack wood, switch over to snow tires, and seal weather stripping against the encroaching chill.

Locals call this time of year "stick season," and it's an apt description. Stick season is when trees stretch their bare limbs heavenward, opening vistas we couldn't see through the leaves. It's a time of revelation that allows light to filter through, when even dense forest views become clear.

Perhaps that's how I'll now try to think of this season—as a time to enjoy fallen leaves like a child, listen to the quiet, and pull darkness around me like a warm quilt. But also, as a time of clearing, of being open to possibility. And in the process, I'll begin to write for myself a new November story.

A MUD-LUSCIOUS WORLD

"How do I love thee, let me count the ways," wrote Elizabeth Barrett Browning. Well, when it comes to spring, it's hard to count the ways and the different voices that have been raised in its praise.

Poets and lovers alike romanticize spring, so it's befitting that April not only ushers in the season but is also the month to honor poetry. Again and again through centuries, poets have tried to capture the sine qua non of spring, the special essence that defines the season.

Rumi, the thirteenth-century Persian poet, described spring as full of "giddiness," a call to play. "In spring," he said, "Don't open the door to the study and begin reading. Take down a musical instrument."

April, Edna St. Vincent Millay wrote, "comes like an idiot, babbling and strewing flowers . . . The sun is hot on my neck . . . The smell of the earth is good." And Gerard Manley Hopkins lifted his pen and voice in wonder, "Nothing is so beautiful as spring," he said, "when weeds, in wheels, shoot long and lovely and lush . . ."

Spring in Vermont, a friend of mine says, is about optimism. But the end of March this year tested my optimism—and my faith. I waited for warmth. I longed in vain for the early tree buds and the serenade of birdsong.

Officially, spring arrives on March 20. But this year, we in the North Country celebrated "spring" not with daisy chains, but in a shower of snowflakes. The cold lingered on and on through the month . . . but now, at last, the snow gods are curling up to sleep and wood nymphs dance again in the valley.

Being optimistic in April really is about holding on, knowing green will return and having the faith to envision it. Faith and hope, those two intangibles. Faith being what the Bible calls the evidence of things not seen; and hope is that intangible mystery that Emily Dickinson described as "the thing with feathers that perches in the soul, and sings the tune without words, and never stops at all."

To me, hope and faith are what spring best represents. And no one better describes this magic than the word magician e e cummings. In his poem "in Just-spring," cummings tells us, "the world is mud-luscious . . ." School boys are shooting marbles and playing pirate; girls are dancing hopscotch and skipping rope. It's just-spring, he says and "the world is puddle-wonderful."

Right now in Vermont it's "just-spring" too. The sap is flowing, the world around us is greening. Winter has huffed its last huff, and warmth curls us in a bear hug. Hope in full bloom, in "just-spring," in Vermont.

SOUNDS OF SPRING

SPRING IS LOUD. NOT BECAUSE STREET SOUNDS INVADE OUR NEWLY opened windows or because the neighborhood chain gang is revving their mowers, chain saws, and Weedwhackers far too early on a Saturday morning.

Spring is loud because it wants our attention. It's nature's alarm clock, jolting us awake from a long winter's nap. The white noise of winter lulls us to sleep during those cold months, when the ground is snuggled beneath a coverlet of snow. In winter, the sun goes to bed early and in the barn, cows dream of open pasture.

But then, after the long frosty silence of winter, there comes a shout—It's spring! Spring in Vermont. The sun tickles the early crocuses, telling them it's time to rise and shine. The peepers sing out their high-pitched chorus, the evening lingers, and birds offer their morning serenade earlier each day.

"Close that book," spring demands, "there's work to do." Get out the rake, head to the garden. No more delay . . . there are windows to wash, the deck to stain, kids who need a ride to Little League. And—of course—there are fish to catch.

It's May, and life is returning in Vermont. Despite the bad press, spring in the North Country is more than just Mud Season. For some, that first signal of spring may be Green Up Day or the eagerly anticipated opening of trout season. For others, it may be Lilac Sunday at the Shelburne Museum or the running of the Burlington Marathon. For me, the sure sign of spring is when the lime-green hue lights the weeping willow near my home.

Each of us has our own special signal of spring's return. And for each of us, the renewal of spring carries a special meaning. Some declare spring is back when the mountain trails are dry enough to hike again. For others it may be the return of bicycle traffic or the reappearance of the neighborhood skateboard jump in the driveway. But you can't hurry the season. Even though the sun shines warmly in March and April, Vermont gardeners know the first frost-free date to safely plant your tomatoes isn't until Memorial Day.

I think Vermont's gift of spring is that it gives us back the carefree days of childhood. The memories of the sweet smell and delicate taste of honeysuckle. The challenge of catching polliwogs, hoping they'll one day grow frog legs. The arrival of languid summer evenings filled with lightning bugs, maple creemees, and staying up until the sun goes down.

A few years ago I learned an important lesson about preconceptions, about seeing and the relativity of beauty. While taking a drive with a Southern relative who had never tasted the eye candy of a Vermont spring, we suddenly had to make an unplanned stop. My cousin jumped out of the car, mesmerized by a sea of yellow in a field of green.

With fresh eyes he looked in awe, much as I had at my first sight of the purple lavender many years ago in Provence. "What," he asked in amazement, "are those flowers? I've never seen them! They're gorgeous!" A bit taken aback, I told him those were dandelions, nuisance weeds that homeowners here consider a scourge. Beauty really is in the eyes of the beholder. And spring lives in our hearts, saying listen, saying stop and look, breathing yes to life's renewal.

HEART AND SOUL

HEART OF VERMONT

January appropriately takes its name from Janus, the two-faced Roman god who looks with one face to the future and the other back to the past. From our vantage point on the cusp of 2012, the new year is a mystery; but 2011 remains vivid in memory as the year of Irene—the year that tested our resiliency and resolve, as individuals and as a state.

By the numbers Vermont is a small state. In total area we rank forty-fifth among the fifty, and by population only Wyoming is smaller. But Vermont has a big state heart. Heaven opened up and poured buckets on us last fall. Rivers raged, swallowed roads, and rearranged town borders. Bridges that had proudly spanned waters for more than a century splintered and floated downstream.

The high pressure of nature's fury tested the strength of Vermont's heart. There were palpitations, there were missed beats, but our pulse remained strong. As a state and as neighbors, we opened our hearts and reached wide our arms to embrace one another.

What is it about human resiliency, about triumph in the face of tragedy? A generation ago, William Faulkner gave us in his novels a testament to the power of the spirit to do more than just survive.

We are immortal, Faulkner said in his Nobel Prize acceptance speech, because we have "a soul, a spirit capable of compassion and sacrifice and endurance." And because of that strength of spirit, Faulkner went on to say, we will not only endure, we will prevail.

Maya Angelou put it another way; she said, "Every one of us has gone to bed one night with fear or pain or loss. And yet each of us has awakened, arisen . . . seen other human beings and said 'Morning, how are you?' 'Fine thanks and you?' Wherever this abides in the human being, there is the nobleness of the human spirit."

While the pictures and memories of the devastation that was Irene are seared into our collective memory, the Vermont response has not been defeat but a resiliency nurtured by compassion. Though on the map our state is small, Vermonters are a bighearted people; and that, not numbers or square miles, is what makes Vermont swell beyond its borders. Vermonters have heart, soul, and spirit in abundance. We know about sacrifice, we reach out with compassion, we nurture hope. And these values, that confidence, tested by the full measure of Irene's wrath, propel us into the future, to not just endure but to prevail.

CULTIVATING KINDNESS

KINDNESS AND *COMPASSION* MAY BECOME THE NEW BUZZ WORDS IN ACA-
demia. With Harvard leading the way, more than two hundred top
colleges and universities are part of a program to revamp the college
admissions process. It's called *Turning the Tide: Inspiring Concern for
Others and the Common Good through College Admissions* and its moniker
is "It's time to say, Enough."

The goal is to shift the focus of the admissions process from being
just about achievement to encouraging more ethical involvement. Or, as
the *Washington Post* headlined its story: "To get into college, Harvard
report advocates for kindness instead of overachieving."

The initiative grew out of a Harvard Graduate Education School
project called "Making Caring Common." The aim is to create a more
humane admissions process by relieving some of the test pressures and
instead encouraging students to be more caring, responsible, and involved
at home and in their communities. The goal is to emphasize values rather
than just academic achievement, and, in the process, help level the playing field for economically disadvantaged students.

Kindness has always been at the top of my value pyramid. The dictionary defines *kindness* as "the ability to show and to live with compassion;
to have, a warm and generous nature, not one that is harsh or likely to
have a destructive effect."

That'ss what poet Mary Oliver meant when she wrote that kindness
is a miracle—a spirit of caring that sets us apart as humans. It's a practice
as well as a value, the ability to reach beyond ourselves to those in need.

Kindness is not just about please-and-thank-you niceties. It's
demonstrated by my friends who open their doors at two in the morning

to children whom the Vermont Department for Children and Families have taken from their own home in the middle of the night. It empowers my sister who works with rescue dogs; a friend who with her therapy dog offers cheer to hospital patients; and a neighbor who on her days off builds houses with Habitat for Humanity.

Kindness and compassion often come from a personal experience with pain or suffering. A recent study found that people who have experienced more adversity are more caring toward others. But you don't have to suffer to have empathy with those who do.

Encouraging students to be more aware of others, to be more sensitive to the challenges facing friends and family, will have long-term societal effects as well as personal benefits. Nurturing compassion, valuing kindness . . . these are lessons colleges are learning, ones they want their students to understand as well.

After all, achievement may be a measure of success, but kindness is the measure of a person.

FINDING HOME

FOR THE FIRST TIME THIS YEAR, I JOINED THE FLOCKS OF WINTER-weary snowbirds and flew south in search of sunshine and warmth. I wanted for at least one brief week to trade the snow of Vermont for the sand of the Gulf. To feel warm without a fleece, to sit seaside in sunshine, nestled into a beach chair with a favorite book for company.

Sunshine and warmth are good for the Vermont body and soul in midwinter. It was two degrees when I boarded the plane in Burlington, just ahead of a major storm. I was in dire need of a refresher course in spring.

After four decades in the North Country, I have acclimated to sub-temperatures. I no longer need to slide plastic bags over my socks to keep my toes warm in my boots, and I can take out the trash without first donning an arctic parka.

It's really about the light, the sun's arc, its rays—and its absence in the long Vermont winter. I admit I need light. Gray pulls me down. Sun shining on my face transforms my countenance, easing the worry lines.

The Beatles, philosopher kings of my generation, understood that special quality of sunshine. "I need to laugh," they sang, "and when the sun is out, I've got something I can laugh about. I feel good, in a special way. I'm in love and it's a sunny day."

But sunshine alone isn't enough. It's a wonderful winter tonic, but it isn't a guarantee of happiness. Recent national studies ranked the Gulf Coast region near bottom when it comes to happiness. But though these sunshine states didn't show up on the radar of contentment, Vermont took high honors as a state of happiness, coming in at number five in two studies.

Even as I was leaving on my jet plane, bags packed and ready to go, I was already looking forward to coming home again. In the movie *Up*, an octogenarian ties his house to a balloon and takes off chasing a dream, only to discover that what is most important are the relationships that nurture us in the place where we are.

The Green Mountains, bidding me good-bye through early-morning haze that day I took flight, were just as welcoming and forgiving when I returned. I admit to wanderlust; I love to travel. But it's always good to come back home to Vermont, where white is the color of winter, green is the hope of spring, and happiness is more than just rays of sun.

Home to Vermont, where my friends are, where my heart beats—back to where my feet always lead me.

COLORING MOMENTS

WINTER SLOWS US DOWN. LIKE THE BEAR AND THE BOBCAT, WE HUMANS look for a place to hibernate in January. We seek a respite after the busyness of the holidays and winter in Vermont offers just that chance.

In January I love waking to the calm of white after a nighttime snowfall has spread a blanket on the world. Even better is when the snowfall surprises as I draw open the curtains. Quiet sometimes speaks louder than words. It's a new year's message saying, "Slow down, you're rushing too fast; don't miss the beauty of this moment."

The process of living consciously in the moment is called mindfulness, and popular culture seems to rediscover it every few years in different guises. One year it's all about yoga, another tai chi, meditation, or feng shui. It may be a best-selling book series about "Cups of Comfort" or a guide to the calming power of decluttering your home. The methods of mindful meditation even include mindful dancing or walking mindfulness.

Of course, this isn't new. For centuries the Japanese have known how to rake a sand garden with precision or prepare tea with the quiet mindfulness of ceremony. The current mindfulness incarnation comes in the form of adult coloring books. According to the online bookseller Amazon, a few years ago a third of the fifteen best-selling books on its site were adult coloring books. Books featuring titles like *Color Me Calm* and *Color Me Happy*, *Coloring Book Mindfulness* and *Anti-Stress Art Therapy for Busy People*.

Even the academic community has chimed in. A study in the journal *Art Therapy* documented the benefit of coloring a mandala as a way to decrease anxiety and manage stress. It was so effective, the study concluded that coloring might be able to ease test-taking anxiety or free us from the fear of flying.

But it's not just academics advocating for mindfulness. There's a growing consensus that mindfulness can so focus our attention on what's happening in the moment, that our mind can be at peace. I think here in Vermont when we slide across a field on cross-country skis or walk in faint moonlight down a snow-covered road, we know a lot about the experience of mindfulness.

I felt that kind of calm on a recent morning as I looked out my French doors to the expanse of white stretching across the back lawn. Brown reeds hugged the edge of a newly frozen stream, rabbit tracks crisscrossed the snow, and the sun almost felt warm, smiling through billowed clouds. Sharing the crystalline quiet of that January morning, I felt completely at peace. It was even better than coloring.

BASEBALL, POETRY & POPCORN

APRIL IS POETRY MONTH. IT IS ALSO THE MONTH TO CELEBRATE empanadas, jugglers, jelly beans, and rubber erasers. Each has its own national celebration day in April. And that's just for openers. There's also National Zucchini Bread Day, Animal Cracker Day, National Garlic Day, Hug an Australian Day, as well as celebrations for caramel popcorn. A month of special interests. A month to remember what we forget to notice.

I guess in our frenetic world we sometimes need to be reminded what it is we love. I love poetry year-round. I love baseball, especially in April, the month in which the hope of October springs eternal. The month in which all things baseball are possible—when thirty teams leave the gate together, a fleeting moment of equal opportunity as each team eyes the prize at the finish line, and the crack of the bat is a sound heard 'round the world.

Spring, baseball, and poetry share a special moment in April. All are the stuff of dreams. Each can inspire us. All three make us feel good about ourselves and the world around us. Spring opens our eyes to fuzz-tufted tree branches; it opens our ears to the serenade of peepers and the sweet melody of songbirds at sunrise. In April we trade in our mittens for fingertips that can feel again. We throw open our doors and welcome in nature. We throw off our hats and shake loose our hair. We get caught up in the madness and willingly play the April fool.

There is no end to the eloquence of poets singing the praises of spring—spring as a glorious time of rebirth, as a metaphor with endless possibilities. Robert Lewis Stevenson wrote both a song to spring and a carol. Conrad Aiken wrote "Nocturne of Remembered Spring," and Robert Frost spoke in poetry, "A Prayer in Spring."

Spring begins to sing in April, so it seems the appropriate time to honor poetry, the chorus of our language. "Oh, to be in England now that April's there," Robert Browning wrote a century ago. But I am happy to celebrate spring in Vermont, a time when the earth awakens to sing an aria and the fields begin to sparkle under a halo of golden sunlight.

Each of us has our own signal of spring. For Frost it was a "darting bird," while poet Katherine Mansfield knew spring was here when "A wind dances over the fields . . . little blue lakes tremble . . . (and) the sun walks in the forest."

For me, the large willow tree that overarches my road speaks spring first. So, too, I add my voice to April's poetry: *Weep no more my willow/ dress up in lemon fringe/sway a tango step/Sweep open wide your arms/welcome the prodigal/home again.*

HOLY CURIOSITY

ONCE AGAIN, ALBERT EINSTEIN BRINGS THE BIGGEST PRESENT TO HIS own birthday party. This March mark 137 years since he was born, deep in the Victorian period of the late 1800s. Last year his birthday was celebrated with a stir, confirming his theory about how we view objects in distant space. This year the day is distinguished by a gift he actually gave the world a century ago, but one that scientists are only now getting around to opening.

For the first time ever, scientists have been able to listen in on the collision of two massive black holes. The collision, which occurred more than a billion years ago, set off a mammoth gravitational sink in space-time, just as Einstein postulated it would a hundred years ago. The physicists know this because they heard what they are calling a "bird chirp" in the universe. And although not usually given to hyperbole, the scientists are saying the discovery is "monumental," that the skies "will never be the same."

All of which has spurred me to think about the nature of genius. Einstein talked a lot about genius, but he called it "imagination." "Imagination is everything," he said. It the "highest form of research." For this particular genius, imagination trumps intellect. Einstein once said that none of his discoveries were ever made through the process of rational thought, but by being inquisitive and embracing the mysterious.

I have a young granddaughter who probably understands Einstein better than most of the adults I know. Her mind is inquisitive, she embraces wonder, and she intuitively knows what the great genius meant when he said, "Creativity is intelligence having fun."

But children too soon grow to adulthood, too often losing their spontaneity, that wonderful creative spark. I think Einstein's real genius was his ability to hold on to these childlike qualities—to forever wonder, to imagine, to keep asking why. Although I'll never really understand the full significance of a gravitational sink in space time, there's still a lot I can learn from Einstein. I can try, like he did, to always be fascinated by riddles and fairy tales, to know the childhood joy of dawdling and the abandon of play, to believe in what cannot be seen.

Like a child, Einstein never lost his awe of the night sky, he never stopped reaching for stars and dreaming dreams. He never stopped asking questions. That is how I understand Einstein's genius and what I take from his legacy.

Or as he himself put it, "Imagination encircles the world . . . Never lose a Holy Curiosity."

MEANDERING

ENTERTAINMENT IN VERMONT COMES NATURALLY. THE GLITZ AND glitter of big-city entertainment is easily accessible just north of the border in Montreal. But in Vermont, pleasures lurk in the slow lane—hiking a mountain path, sailing solitary on the lake, romancing a walleye, or floating a kayak down a river.

Vermont is an outdoor state. Even though the nip of frost comes in late October and hovers through early May, we Vermonters take our cue in winter, not from the hibernating black bear but from a whitetail deer or a pesky beaver. We prefer to play in winter rather than roll up in a ball and sleep away the season. There are fields to snowshoe, woodland trails to cross-country ski, mountains to downhill, or lanes to ride a snowmobile. And most communities have an ice rink for the local hockey crew.

When spring finally peeks out in May, it rewards our tenacity and renews our faith. Life in the meadows begins to return. But it's in early June that Vermont really awakens. When buds suddenly bathe the trees, brown turns green, and pink appears petal-soft on backyard fruit trees. By mid-June, the lime green of spring matures into emerald, the birthstone of summer, and Vermont earns its nickname as the "Green Mountain State."

In June I love to head out on a lazy search of Vermont. To meander. There's a fine art to meandering, going nowhere in particular and not being in a hurry to get there. Meandering, like meditation, takes patience and practice. The adventure is in the journey, and the journey is the destination.

Recently I spent twenty-four hours in Montreal. It was a whirlwind in a day. A cacophony of life with art on the sidewalk, theater in the street, and buildings scraping the sky. People—and time—rushing by. Loud and raucous.

It was indeed exciting, and, I admit, at least once or twice a year I need that urban adventure. But how different the day was from my usual weekend meandering in Vermont. On my woods walk the only chatter I hear comes from birds gossiping in the trees. The rush is from a brook whooshing by, and the bustle and busyness are the scurrying of insects burrowing a fallen tree stump.

A day in Vermont is green by natural design. It is illumined by sunlight rather than neon signs. Time loses meaning, minutes blend into hours, and I am at peace.

It was in the 1950s that everything seemed to go "instant"—instant rice, instant coffee, frozen dinners. In response, Simon and Garfunkel told us in the 1960s, "Slow down, you move too fast, you've got to make the morning last . . ."

I think that making the morning, the moment, last is one of the things we do best here in Vermont. And so, this weekend, I won't be border crossing in search of merriment. I'll be meandering locally, off in search of Vermont, where getting lost means finding something special.

VERMONT TRUE

IN SEARCH OF VERMONT

I HAD A FRIEND ONCE WHO CALLED VERMONT A PRETEND STATE. HE said that the state tourist office plants the meadows with wildflowers in spring, hires cows who moo on cue, infuses the Green Mountains with chlorophyll every summer, and carts snow in from Canada to blanket the winter hillsides.

That friend has long since moved away. But I often think of his notion that Vermont offers a Bob Newhart country inn view of life. It's true that tourists—and often flatlanders—flock here in search of nostalgia, looking for a simpler life, for old-time values, and scenic vistas. But the reality of Vermont is more complicated than that and far richer. Vermont is a state with many faces and multiple personalities.

A few weeks ago I headed out on my annual leaf-peeping tour, following the out-of-state license plates down Route 7, through Middlebury Gap, and north on Route 100. I stopped at the country store in Ripton, had homemade pie and ice cream in Rochester, and this year added a local winery to my itinerary, sampling some Vermont fruit of the vine. I felt fortunate to call this special place my home.

But I will always think of myself as an interloper here, a flatlander. Though I've lived here more than forty years, I'm not a native. I didn't grow tall in mountain country. I moved here from flat land "down south" in Washington, DC. But recently I took a late-autumn ride with someone who can call himself a real Vermonter, someone whose roots sink generations deep into Vermont soil. And now I understand a little better the difference between a born Vermonter and an adopted one like me.

My friend and I walked through the small local cemetery in Bakersfield where his grandparents are buried, and then we went in search of the field where their dairy farm once stood. We drove past the Underhill house that was my friend's first home with his young family.

We also stopped in Jeffersonville to wander the deserted yard of Dr. Mann's Hospital. Dr. Roger Mann died not long ago at the age of 103. Over the decades, countless Vermont children, including my friend, were born in that three-story white clapboard house that served as a way station and rural hospital.

On that day trip retracing roots, my friend shared a piece of real Vermont and the love he has for his forebearers and this state he still calls home. It's the story of a place that, for those born here, is not imaginary or pretend, not just picturesque and idyllic. Vermont is a very real place, their home state, where they grew up, and their parents, and their parents' parents. A place they affectionately call home. And now, so do I.

HARVEST SUPPER

WHAT DOES IT TAKE TO FEED SIX HUNDRED HUNGRY PEOPLE? NINETY chickens; ninety-three dessert pies; hundreds of pounds of potatoes, squash, and cabbage; a large church kitchen; and a whole lot of organization. That was a recipe for success at the seventy-first annual chicken pie supper at the Richmond Congregational Church in early November. Chickens, pies, potatoes, and an army of well over one hundred volunteers preparing a harvest feast.

Fall is full of seasonal activities in Vermont. The October calendar fills up fast with apple orchard events, corn mazes, haunted forests, hayrides, and visits to the pumpkin patch. But for me, nothing captures the season better than the local community tradition of church chicken pie suppers. And no, they aren't dinners, they're suppers. Not a formal affair, just friends, neighbors, and families sitting down together for a pre-Thanksgiving community feast to share and celebrate fall's bounty.

From Newport to North Danville, from Hinesburg to Jericho, and Groton to Berlin, friends, families and strangers celebrate the fall harvest and foliage season by gathering for supper. It's a rich tradition that in some communities dates back more than a hundred years.

These local chicken pie suppers hold a special place in my heart and in the life of our family. The events are popular, and reservations are best made well in advance. On the evening of the event, hungry patrons line the church steps waiting for their "seating" to be called. It usually takes two or three seatings to accommodate everyone.

These suppers are family affairs, and once again there were three generations of our family sitting together. But this year the numbers will swell. We'll need an extra-long table, because arriving just in time for supper are out-of-town relatives from Philadelphia and Florida.

It doesn't really matter whether it's Richmond or Hinesburg or Jericho, the menu and style of the church chicken pie suppers are likely to be the same. Everyone sits elbow to elbow at long tables laden family style with plates of biscuit-topped chicken pie; bowls of mashed potatoes, squash, coleslaw, and cranberry sauce; and, of course, rich gravy. And once the plates are cleared, out come the coffee and homemade pies—your choice of apple or pumpkin—accompanied by a wedge of cheddar cheese.

It's local Vermont at its very best, an event our family eagerly awaits each autumn. As I walked out of the church after supper a few weeks ago, satiated and happy, I couldn't help thinking of Mae West's wry wisdom: "Too much of a good thing can be wonderful."

FIDDLING TIME

ON A RAINY SATURDAY NIGHT IN APRIL, I DROVE UP THE INTERSTATE with friends to celebrate my favorite end-of-winter, early spring event— the St. Albans Maple Festival Fiddlers Variety Show, a uniquely North- western Vermont event, mixing music and community with a flair of "just across the border."

The names on the program—Gaston and Guy, Fabio and Michelle, Latimer and Roland—gave a hint of the event's mixed lineage. French is spoken as freely as English, but what is shared, what makes the eve- ning special, is the music. And it's translatable into any language—jigs and reels, waltzes and quadrilles—all toe-tapping, energetic, and infec- tious fun.

As we passed Exit 18 on our way north, my friends told me that for years they came here to Georgia to the Cobweb Dance Hall. On a Sat- urday night it was the place to be for round dancing and square dancing, and, oh yes—BYOB, No Shorts, and Families Welcome. It was also a cross-border event with that same brand of hoedown fiddling.

The Cobweb doesn't sit just off the interstate anymore. It's long gone, but the tradition of old-time music is still very much alive in Northern Vermont. It's a tradition that brings together generations. This year, the St. Albans Fiddlers Show moved from its usual stage at the local high school academy to St. Paul's Methodist Church, because the school audi- torium is—thankfully—undergoing renovation.

The church hall was packed with well over a hundred people. There was a diverse mix of beard lengths, hair colors, and boot sizes coming together. A shared space for women and men, the young and not so young, fiddlers, cloggers, piano plunkers, and singers.

There was recognizable music—"The Tennessee Waltz," "Turkey in the Straw," and "Comin''Round the Mountain"—and some little-known tunes with evocative names such as "Turkey in the Patch," "Hamish the Carpenter," and "Chinese Breakdown." I don't really know the difference between a waltz and a reel, but it didn't matter that evening.

I do know there was an intriguing range of instruments—fiddles of course (all sizes), guitars and piano for backup, harmonicas (small and considerably larger), and this year's surprise addition—bagpipes serenading at intermission.

All the music seemed to be variations on a tune, the influences and nationalities like the United Nations—Gaelic, Scottish, Quebecois, and a little Kentucky bluegrass. I recognized from previous years some of the same songs, many of the same faces, even a few of the same outfits—like Dave's red suspenders and Roger's Irish cable sweater.

The program was considerably shorter this year, just under three hours, rather than ringing in midnight. But there was no lack of camaraderie or lowdown-hoedown fun. It's a worthy down-home tradition in upstate Vermont—a fiddlers' variety that ushers out winter and welcomes in spring.

JOE'S POND

THE ICE ON JOE'S POND DOMINATES LATE-WINTER CONVERSATION IN the Northeast Kingdom town of West Danville. The pond froze over shortly after Thanksgiving this year, and by New Year's Day the ice measured fourteen inches. But it's the ice melt that everyone is anticipating.

Over the months-long stretch of winter, as many as twelve thousand pundits worldwide will try to guess the precise moment a cinder block plunges through the ice on Joe's Pond, declaring the official end to winter in Vermont.

The Joe's Pond Ice-Out Contest is part of the local seasonal folklore, an antidote to cabin fever. It's been going on for nearly three decades. The rules are simple, the technology lowbrow, and the tickets cheap. It still takes only a dollar to wager on the time of the block's plunge—the same cost of a ticket when the contest first began more than thirty years ago.

It was in the late 1980s, during a long stretch of cabin fever, that a group of friends came up with the idea for the ice-out contest. The men frequently met for morning coffee at Joe's Pond Country Store and talk inevitably turned to the weather. The question on everyone's mind was the same: "When will the ice on the pond go out?"

One morning the men decided to wager on the date of the ice-out, and the contest was born. But the big challenge was to come up with a method marking the precise time of the lake thaw. The system the men devised had a backwoods beauty in its simplicity, and it remains in place with only a few modifications.

An electric clock is placed on a wooden pallet connected by wire to a cinder block one hundred feet out on the pond. When the cinder block cracks through the ice, the clock is dislodged and the "official" time of the ice-out is recorded. The wager closest to the date and time wins. Most winners have been Vermonters, though wagers come from around the world. Proceeds are split 50/50 with the Joe's Pond Committee, which uses its share to fund the town's Fourth of July fireworks.

It's a case of small pleasures bringing big rewards. The annual Joe's Pond Ice-Out has become part of the warp and woof of this Vermont kingdom town. Part legend, mostly fun, the contest helps West Danville residents survive the subzero days of winter until green returns to the mountainsides. That's when Joe's Pond again twinkles in the sunlight shimmer of summer and locals gather to watch the heavens ignite in early July.

MAIL CALL

THE POSTAL SERVICE IS OFTEN A POPULAR FISCAL FLOGGING POST FOR Washington politicians. But according to a recent Gallop poll, 74 percent of the American public rate the post office the most trusted federal agency. And I agree.

These days, I only get "real mail" twice a year . . . by that I mean something with my name handwritten on the envelope. But it's a delivery I anticipate—and treasure.

Every six months—at Christmas and for my summer solstice birthday—envelopes appear in my mailbox like manna from heaven. Inside are cards and letters from people who actually know me and took the trouble to go out and buy a stamp—keepsake communiques from friends with the personal touch of actual penmanship.

The mail means a lot; it brings that human touch of connection. But so too does mail delivery. For years my mother waited in her porch rocker for the afternoon mail. It wasn't just about the mail; it was about a friendly face and a few minutes of conversation for an older woman living alone. Now, I too am older and appreciate the familiar smile of my mail delivery person.

For me, there's also a mystique about the postal service and its colorful history. The system of post offices crisscrossing the nation was the brainchild of Ben Franklin, one of my historical heroes. And the exploits of the Pony Express have always captured my imagination, as has the postal service's informal credo that neither "snow nor rain nor heat nor gloom of night" will "stay" couriers from their appointed rounds.

According to research by Vermont's Brookfield Historical Society, the state's early postal delivery was a rural version of the Pony Express.

Horses with names like Daisy, Ned, Bell, and Bess carried the mail, stopping at every mailbox on their route, even on the Sabbath.

Most legendary in the Brookfield postal stable was Old Gray. Over thirteen years of service, Old Gray logged more than fifty thousand miles of mail delivery—enough to circle the earth twice. And that pony delivery tradition continued, off and on, until the early 1940s, because horses could get through drifting snow and spring mud when vehicles with tires couldn't.

My mail is delivered now not by horseback, but by a white van with a blue eagle. Yet it still brings a sense of anticipation. Each day is a surprise as I leaf through a handful of bills and flyers. Who knows, maybe tucked somewhere in the middle will be a picture postcard from a friend on summer vacation, writing, "Having a great time, wish you were here."

RIPENING TOMATOES

"THE TOMATOES ARE PLUMPING, THE CUKES ARE PROLIFIC, AND THE acorn squash abundant." No, I'm not talking about here in Vermont, not yet anyway. Up here, late winter is just beginning to segue into early spring. Maple sugaring time is barely over and mud season still, well, muddy.

But my long-time Vermont neighbors write of backyard bounty in their new Florida homestead. The proprietors of the many acre garden just down the road from me have moved out of sight of Mount Mansfield. They've relocated to a climate where the seasons are all askew. Where vegetables ripen early and wither in midsummer heat, just as we in Vermont are harvesting our gardens' abundance.

My farmer friends have happily fled the ice and snow of Vermont winters to settle into a life that moves at a different pace, to a place with sun warmth in January and garden tomatoes in April. But though I, too, enjoy a visit south in frigid February, I've opted to keep my roots deep here in Vermont.

The truth is, I'm used to tomatoes in August, and I really do like the snow that transforms winter days to crystal. I like roads less traveled, human-size towns, herds of Holsteins, and the many shades of green surrounding me as I meander down backroads. I like chance encounters with woodland creatures as I wander trails in early spring, and I love the profusion of trillium in Burlington's Red Rocks Park on Mother's Day.

I think what I treasure most here in my home place is the change and diversity of our landscape—the expectation, the anticipation, the changing seasons offer. Autumn is a rich artist's palette, a cacophony of color. Summer waves at me with its vibrant, undulating green, and winter pulls a soft coverlet of white around my shoulders. And nothing can match spring in Vermont, young and rambunctious, a riot of laughing sounds and colors. Stepping into the sunlight after long months of cold and hibernation, spring offers us the hope of rebirth, the wonder of renewal.

The best songs of life-come-again are the wetland symphony of peepers in the early evening and the quiet chorus of doves in the morning. I'm excited by the first welcome sighting of a rusty-chested robin tugging at a worm on my back lawn, and the lime-green sway of nearby weeping willows. And I'm still transfixed by the subtle way green seeps back into the grass early each spring and buds kiss open the tips of bare branches.

To my transplanted friends, I'll concede the warmth of their southern winter and the harvest of early spring tomatoes. But give me the seasons that shift and surprise me, that are the calendar of my life. I'll savor spring in my Green Mountain home, with buds, returning robins, and the cows back out in the pasture. I'll watch vegetable seedlings grow in my window greenhouse, and I'll await with expectation the ripening of tomatoes—in August.

CLOUDY, SEXY VERMONT

THANKS TO MY EXTENDED CABLE PACKAGE, I WATCH THE SUN RISE GLO-
riously every morning. *Sunrise Earth* is beamed in vivid color and
high-definition clarity on my television screen. I see a different sunrise
from a different location to start the day, which is a good thing, because
in Vermont the sun doesn't rise most mornings—or so it seems.

Burlington's cloud cover is the state tourist agency's best-kept secret.
A cover-up worthy of Nixon and Watergate. It's a little-known fact, but
ranking just below Seattle, Burlington has the second-fewest sunny days
in the country. It's a top designation we Vermonters would rather not talk
about. Like the fact that, according to *Men's Health* magazine, Burlington
is the second-least-sexy city in America.

Thanks to that miracle of TV, I can ignore the gloom outside my
window and on an overcast morning watch the sun on *Sunrise Earth*
climb above a mountain ridge in Tibet or cast a pink net deep into the
Florida Everglades.

On a recent morning, as I watched an enormous sun shimmer out
of the ocean, small letters on the TV screen gave me some perspective.
Sunrise that morning was beamed from Australia's Great Coral Reef,
where there are no seasons, because the sun sits so high in the sky. The
same sun that nurtures a richly diverse aqua system makes land boring
in its sameness.

My sister has lived in Florida close to half a century, nearly as long as
I have been in Vermont. She loves the mild climate there, but she admits
what she misses in that temperate fantasyland are the changing seasons.
While here in the North we witness dramatic seasonal personalities, in
the South the months seem to just segue into each other.

As I breathe in the aphrodisiac of autumn air and reflect, I think Burlington really is pretty sexy.

Even as the chlorophyll weeps out of Vermont's sugar maples, the mountainsides ignite in a blaze of sizzling orange, lemon zest, and sparkling burgundy. If I look east to the mountains, I can see the flapping skirts of Moulin Rouge dancers and hear the squawking geese announce a wardrobe change.

Sunlight is contracting now, November and December approach with their short days and heart of darkness. Fortunately, when I get up in the black night of daybreak, I can turn the sun on and watch it rise seductively on TV. In dreary midday, I can turn on my full-spectrum lamp to make light of my seasonal affective disorder.

In other words, I have ways of coping with seasonal dysfunction. I can bring light into my life here in cloudy Vermont; but the only way my sister in Florida can capture the smell of autumn air and the crunch of falling leaves is to hop on a plane and come visit me.

I'm not exactly sure who is keeping track and passing judgment, but I think Vermont is a seasonal cornucopia and a very sexy place to live, after all.

FAMILY TIES

YES!

SOME THINGS NEVER DISAPPOINT. I FIRST VISITED PARIS MORE THAN four decades ago. Last fall, I returned, filled with anticipation, but fearing disappointment. Afraid that the Paris of reality wouldn't live up to the Paris of memory. But Paris doesn't disappoint, and even though the monuments are so familiar that they are almost clichés, you can't help but be awestruck by their magnificence.

I thought about that a few weeks ago when my granddaughter was born. Every day almost four hundred thousand babies are born worldwide, yet each birth, each baby, holds its own aura, its own magnificence. Each birth offers hope, and each baby reinforces for me the incredible potential of one, the power of one.

Both my sons live in the rarified air inside the Beltway that rings Washington, DC. When the talk turns to politics, they speak with passion and energy. The same passion I once had; the belief in change that once energized me. With age I have become weary and perhaps a little wiser. I now believe positive change only comes one by one by one, in the power of one passing it on, the power of one uniting with others. Like the courageous individuals joining together throughout the Arab world during the Arab Spring of the early 2010s, passing on the power to say no to repression. And those in towns and cities across the United States who stood tall and asserted Black Lives Matter.

When I worked as a public interest advocate in Washington in the 1980s, I was inspired by a regal, soft-spoken woman, Esther Peterson, the grande dame of the consumer movement. She was untiring in her efforts to give a voice to the voiceless. A friend of mine told me of a visit she made shortly before Esther passed away. This woman, who initiated more tangible positive change than most of us dream of, was pained by nagging doubt. "Did I . . ." she asked my friend, "did I really make a difference?"

I believe that is what most of us want to leave as our legacy. Did I make a difference? Is the world a better place because I passed by? I believe our power of change is the power of one, each of us doing a small part. The power of one to mentor, to volunteer, to reach out to a neighbor in need, to offer encouragement and understanding, to show kindness. These small steps, the ones we often take for granted, are the real giant leaps for mankind.

So yes, my granddaughter Eliza is a beautiful little girl. And yes, she represents hope. Yes, she joins the army of the next generation born the same February night she was—the night of the full moon opening on the dawn of what I hope will be a more compassionate world. So that her voice of one will be lifted up with others born that night, and with Molly Bloom, who in the final chapter of *Ulysses* so powerfully affirms life with her "yes, yes, a thousand times . . . yes!"

WEATHER OR NOT

I'VE OFTEN WONDERED WHY WEATHER FORECASTERS SEEM SO HAPPY. Perhaps banter and grin are a required course freshman year. Or bubbly is a prerequisite for weather school admission.

Secretly, I've always harbored a desire to be a weatherperson. Even now I linger by the mounted thermometer display in the hardware store. For years I followed the vagaries of the west wind with a four-way weather station mounted on my back deck that not only gauged temperature and rainfall, but wind speed and direction. It did practically everything but feed the birds.

I know plastic is low-tech, and my weather port doesn't do protracted ten-day forecasts, but I think it's every bit as reliable as Super Doppler Radar. For that matter, so is my back door that opens to the heavens and accurately detects rainfall; and my arthritic knees don't need electronic sensors to know when the barometric pressure is falling.

Still, I hold weatherpeople in awe. I can only imagine how grand it must be to don a tux and top hat once a year and cuddle a furry groundhog while the whole country waits in anticipation of a shadow.

Maybe you do have to be all smiles when you're predicting something as fickle as the weather. But where is the accountability? Even sportscasters are often called upon to stand by their predictions and admit when their rankings have gone awry. I guess it's just too hard to hold anyone accountable for the eccentricity of clouds.

In the name of weather, though, I can forgive almost anything. My family has a long tradition of weather fascination. My grandfather spent sixty years of his life chronicling the morning and evening temperatures and weather conditions outside his living room window in Lakemont,

Pennsylvania. His legacy when he passed on was boxes full of composition notebooks with black marbled covers and line after line of detailed weather data—plus a brief notation marking the date and hour of a new grandchild's birth.

Frankly, in my family there wouldn't be much talk if it weren't for the weather. Weather is the grease of our family conversation wheel. Whether it's hot and humid, drizzling, damp, or sunny, weather fills in the pauses. When all else fails, weather can placate and unite us.

As soon as the first warnings of a major snow event in Vermont are broadcast, the phone lines start hopping from my family in Philadelphia and Florida wanting to know if I'm snowed in—and do I have enough food. In return, I'm on the line during hurricane season in the Gulf Coast, checking on family. And when DC is hot enough to fry eggs on the asphalt, I am channeling my sons, asking if their air conditioners are in good repair.

Let's face it, nimbus and cumulus clouds are a lot easier to talk about than feelings. If the conversation takes a serious turn over the Thanksgiving turkey, my brother will always save the day by bringing up the wind. Storms trump controversy, and the heat index is a lot less of a hot topic than politics.

Still, I have this fantasy that one night the weatherperson on the six o'clock news will stand in front of his virtual TV storm map, turn to the news anchor, and, with a straight face, ask: "And how are you really feeling tonight?" It's a scary thought . . . whether it ever happens or not.

GOOD NIGHT, VERMONT

I AM THE MOTHER OF SONS. IDENTICAL TWINS NOW IN THEIR MID-
thirties. They are men I will always call my boys; I will always carry
memories of the little cars and action figures they carried in their pock-
ets when they were five—and four and seven. Miniature cars and plastic
superheroes that for years peopled the bottom of my purse and churned
through the washing machine.

But now I have a granddaughter. The pot of blond hair at the end of
the rainbow. An endearing smile, a constant joy. Jet lag and withdrawal
after a recent journey are a small price to pay to spend time with her. To
reconnect with family, to renew our love. To carry a little bit of Vermont
to just outside the nation's capital.

Whenever I visit my sons, I take as much Vermont with me as I
can. They have Vermont bumper stickers on their cars and proudly wear
the UVM logo on their baseball caps and T-shirts. Though they weren't
actually born here, they have Green Mountain grass growing between
their toes, and Vermont is the only home they know. From a distance
they join fellow expatriates in Washington and cheer on the UVM men's
basketball team during the opening moments of March Madness, proud
of their connection to the Green Mountain state.

En route to a DC visit, I stuff Vermont-made pepperoni into my
carry-on, along with a T-shirt from a Vermont vineyard for one son and
a baseball cap from a local brewery for the other. I tote newspaper articles
about a new barbecue restaurant in Waterbury and the new brewpub in
Shelburne, just down the road from where they grew up.

What is a visit from a Vermont mom without a taste of home? Taking Green Mountain magic to far-off sons whose hearts will always be

green and feet forever rooted in the black soil of home. My heart is filled with Vermont connections and with the hope that my granddaughter will come to know what makes this tiny state such a special place.

In the evening, when I tuck her into bed, we read together the board book by Michael Tougias that whispers, "Goodnight Vermont"—"Don't you love the fresh mountain air? Good evening, woods and stone wall. Good evening, friends."

Even when I'm far away, my heart brings me back to my Vermont home, not the home of my birth but the home of my soul, where my roots have taken hold and where my sons grew strong and tall, their characters nurtured and honed by Vermont values.

My granddaughter may never call the Green Mountains of Vermont home, but I hope as she grows, she will know as more than just pictures in a book the valleys and brooks of Vermont, the country roads, and the dairy cows and baby moose.

That she will breathe fresh mountain air, play in messy mud season, and say with the author of the book, "Thank you, Vermont for sharing a wonderful day."

THANKS AND GIVING

I'm hosting pilgrims from Plymouth this Thanksgiving. Well, actually, it's my in-laws on a pilgrimage from their home near the Massachusetts Rock, crossing miles and states to spend the holiday here in Vermont. Also coming over the river and through the woods are my children from Maryland and Virginia, and, for her first Thanksgiving feast, a new granddaughter. All of which adds up to a lot to be thankful for this year.

When I think what it is I'm thankful for, my list is long. I'm thankful for my titanium knees that can now hike Camel's Hump. I'm thankful for my eyes that after cataract surgery can see clearly the Green Mountains silhouetted in the eastern sky. I'm thankful for the connection of friends and family; I'm thankful for brown-basted turkeys and pies of any kind; and I'm thankful for the little everyday things that we mostly take for granted—those wonderful random acts of kindness that we sometimes forget to count among our blessings.

I'm thankful for the store clerk who smiles patiently as I fumble for the right change and for the neighbor who leaves a Tupperware container by my front door with a generous serving of still-simmering squash soup. I'm thankful for a telephone call from a friend just saying hello and for a late-night rambling conversation with the young man next door when we meet by the recycle bins.

I'm thankful for the teenage girl who helped load my groceries in the car trunk on a rainy night and for my garage man, who rescues me but doesn't lecture when I chew my front tire to the rim, believing futilely that it would make it whole to his shop.

I'm thankful for all the people who are going to be in churches and local restaurants today dishing up mashed potatoes and serving cranberry sauce, thankful for the people who are handing out warm winter coats and for those who donated them, and thankful for people who are taking a little time out of their family day to visit someone alone in a nursing home.

All the special people who do special things, not expecting anything special in return. Those very special people who are generous in spirit and understand that the word *charity* really means more than merely giving, it means love.

When generations and blended families gather around our Thanksgiving table this year, you'll need a genealogy tree to tell who is who and how everyone fits in. And with us this year will also be a couple from a continent far away, unrelated to anyone at the table. A couple from Kenya is joining us in the time-honored American tradition of turkey and stuffing, coleslaw, mashed potatoes, and pumpkin pie. Joining with us because our hosts, my ex-husband and his partner, understand that giving is what thanks is all about.

COWS AND CLEAN AIR

Excitement brims! After years of planning and dreaming, false starts and delays, my son, daughter-in-law, and two young granddaughters are heading home to Vermont. They're choosing, as my husband and I did thirty-plus years ago, to move north to raise their family, trading the fast track for the slow lane. They're fleeing the big city of Washington, DC, to settle down here in Vermont, choosing the not-quite-great lake to call home.

For me, it's a dream come true. That dream of every grandparent to have family close by. No more problematic plane flights and weather delays to visit my "kids." No need now to reintroduce myself to my granddaughters after a six-month hiatus. Kudos to my son and his wife for pulling it off, for finding a way to make the move—finally—happen.

But then I drive down Shelburne Road at six o'clock in the evening, dawdling in traffic, thankful for the radio to help me make it through "rush hour." I sit at a red light reflecting on all the cars on the road and the fact that the infrastructure just isn't adequate for the crush of traffic. I remember the nearly deserted state I moved to in the early 1980s, and I mutter, "*Close the floodgates, halt the influx of flatlanders.*" Then, of course, I catch myself and add, "*Well, stop the migration once my family has safely arrived.*"

I know it's not a perfect world, and in moving from urban Washington, DC, to semirural Vermont, my son and his family will be exchanging one set of problems for another. Vermont is not the same place I moved to with my young family. The state hasn't escaped the epidemic of drug abuse and all its spin-off problems. The cost of housing here, of food, of heating—the costs of living in Vermont—can be daunting. And the tax burden is onerous, one of the highest in the country, while well-paid professional job opportunities are limited.

But long ago I decided life is about trade-offs, about the road taken rather than the road not taken. Well before she knew she was going to relocate, my three-year-old granddaughter decided she wanted to be a tractor driver when she grew up. Now she's thrilled to know that whenever she wants, she can visit the cows and farm animals at Shelburne Farms and the chickens, pigs, and perhaps a summer lamb that a friend raises in Warren.

My granddaughter did go blueberry picking last summer, and she's expert at building snowmen and making the most wonderful snow angels. But she hasn't tried on skis or ice skates yet, she hasn't gone to mud camp at the Audubon Center, tasted sugar on snow—and so much more that lies in wait.

To the happy wanderers, I open my arms and my heart and say, "Welcome home."

CHRISTMAS PRESENT

CHRISTMAS IN THE MIDDLE OF THE LAST CENTURY—WHAT A FRIGHT-ening way to describe my childhood holiday. It was the 1950s, the era of the Slinky and pink aluminum Christmas trees, a time warp before microchips ruled the world, when the only movement under the tree was a Lionel train that was off the track more than it was on.

My Christmas Past arrived with Santa in the downtown Thanksgiving Day parade and the fat Sears, Roebuck and Company catalog in the mail. That marvel of merchandising was called the "Wish Book," and it stirred high excitement, causing visions of far more than sugar plums to dance in children's heads.

Early December followed with the unveiling of extravagant department store window displays. Out with the manikins and in with glitter and glamour as Gimbels tried to out-glitz rival store Lits, and neither was able to compete with Wanamakers.

At least that's how it was in Philadelphia.

And why, you may ask, should anyone care about my stories of Christmas Past? My sons raise the same question with their eyebrows and a groan. Maybe it's that Christmas is the calendar keeping track of our lives, the red Salvation Army kettle of memories.

I don't remember much about the first day of kindergarten, but I do remember that hard rubber doll with the fixed expression of innocence I received one Christmas morning. And the sidewalk roller skates a few Christmases later; the year of my fingerprint spy kit; and especially the Christmas-morning excitement of receiving T. S. Eliot's *Collected Poems* when I was eighteen. I still have that gift, and also the memories of my sons' Big Wheels Christmas, the year of our first dog, Peter S. Beagle, and our first Christmas in Vermont.

Christmas is a magical memory machine. We crank it up and ask for joy and good cheer. It's easy to say that my Christmas Past was a simpler, better time—which is what, twenty years from now, my children will probably be telling their children. It's the myth we all want to believe. We don't want to dwell on the inevitable Christmas disappointments, the sadness the season can bring. We want to keep alive dreams of sleighs filled with toys and snowmen that dance, so we work hard to create memories that will overflow the chimney stockings of Christmas Future.

But there's a funny thing about memories. The best ones aren't always those at which we've worked the hardest. Often, they're the ones we stumble upon, the ones we pick up along the way without intending to.

One of our family's favorite holiday tales is about the year our cat managed to topple the holiday tree not once but twice, as well as the saga of the sweet potato casserole my mother-in-law dropped en route to the Christmas table. It's in this morning of the present where we really find the future memories of Christmas Past.

May your Christmas be filled with wonder and memories—intended or not.

A FULLNESS OF FAMILY

SUMMER ENDED FOR ME THIS YEAR WITH A GATHERING OF FAMILY AT A lake house on South Hero Island in Lake Champlain. It was a modern family reunion—a family connected by more than blood lines. A family with an unconventional family tree, but one with deep roots and branches stretching wide.

Three generations gathered from across the United States and down from Canada for this get-together. There were kids—cousins sharing laughter if not chromosomes—spouses, partners, exes, and lots of dogs. Yet somehow it all worked, it all blended, and I felt surrounded by abundance.

Which led me to mull the question: Just how do you define family? If you define it by caring and sharing—by love—then this was a family. Gay, straight, young, old, children by a current marriage or a previous one—somehow it didn't really matter. No one was keeping score.

In some ways, this felt like the set for the TV series *Modern Family*, without all the dysfunction. Gathered at the house by the lake were a stay-at-home mom and a stay-at-home dad. There was an array of aging but energetic baby boomers and a younger generation that included a lawyer, an engineer, a teacher, an environmental consultant, and . . . did I forget anyone?

The food ranged from Italian to Mexican, vegetarian to barbeque; the drinks from cosmos to mineral water. The kids and the dogs came in a variety of sizes and ages, and the house was a way station for relatives and friends. It all felt like a dictionary definition of *fullness*—"filled to capacity; holding as much or as many as is possible."

But the fullness I experienced that week by the lake was measured by more than numbers and mixtures, more than just variety and diversity. The fullness was characterized by abundance, by richness. By happiness, contentment, and connection.

Being a wordsmith, I decided to investigate this word *fullness*, to find out more about its origins and meanings—to check out its genealogy. The word, meaning "plenty," can be traced to fifteenth-century French, and it has a long dictionary list of meanings.

There is *full*, meaning "whole, lacking nothing"; *full*, meaning "to eat enough"; and *full*, as in "to live a full life." A "full" moon shone down on us that week in late August, and, as described by the final dictionary entry, "We left the place with full hearts." I chose to follow the genealogy of the word *fullness* rather than dig into definitions of *family*, because I didn't need a dictionary to tell me that this gathering I was privileged to be part of was family. How much better the word *fullness* captured the nuances of our time together, this gathering of my very special "family."

Nature Walk

BIRDSONG

I LOVE HEARING THE BIRDS IN SPRING. THEIR BACKYARD SERENADE greets me in the morning, inviting me to share their symphony. Chirps, chatters, warbles and caws are music to my ears. The sights and sounds of returning birds combine into a festive rite of spring.

Whenever I venture beyond the backyard into the nearby woods, I listen especially closely for the lilting voice of a local hermit thrush. Like many other Vermonters, this neighbor winters in the South but returns to Vermont every spring. It's our official state bird, and it breeds and raises its young here, so they're real Vermonters—true natives!

The hermit thrush is a songbird that lives in the evergreen and hardwood forests of all fourteen Vermont counties. Indigenous legend has it that in the first days, the thrush had no voice. But while other vociferous birds squabbled among themselves, the thrush was busy ridding the forest of insects. As a reward for its hard work and gentle nature, the hermit thrush was given a beautiful voice and a melodic song.

Songbirds are both the color and voice of the forest. It's hard to imagine a backwoods hike that doesn't mix silence and solitude with the sound, the music of songbirds. Forests blanket three fourths of the state of Vermont, and they're home to more than two hundred species of birds, including a wide variety of songbirds.

Yet songbirds head the list of the avian population gradually disappearing from Vermont's forests. According to a report by the Norwich-based Vermont Center for Ecostudies, much of our bird population is in decline. Particularly hard hit are species that live on flying insects—including many songbirds as well as other insectivores. Fortunately, though, the hermit thrush population has been able to remain robust.

Our birds and wooded areas are a gift of the Vermont landscape and a special part of our heritage. To see the flash of a goldfinch, to stand in the royal presence of a red-robed cardinal, or to be treated to a chorus of woodland songbirds is to be reminded of our bond with nature.

After all, we too sing to each other out of love—just like the birds—who sing, the poet Sharon Olds tells, from "love of sound . . . love of other birds . . . love of singing itself."

TREE CITY VERMONT

My son isn't known for being on the cutting edge of the twenty-first century. He eschews technology, reads the environmental poet Wendell Berry, and for relaxation goes winter camping.

When he moved back to Vermont a few years ago, he hoped for woods, not suburbia. To his chagrin, he ended up down the road from Taft's Corner, the shopping mecca of Chittenden County. He's been planting trees ever since, in every corner of his yard—which may actually put him on the cutting edge after all.

According to a report in a recent issue of *Science* magazine, the answer to global warming is planting trees—a trillion of them all around the globe. The study calculated the new trees, in just a few decades, would suck up more than eight hundred billion tons of carbon dioxide. That's a significant shrinking of the world's carbon footprint, and according to the study's author, would be "by far—by thousands of times—the cheapest climate change solution."

And it's not just about climate control. Trees also cut costs for energy consumption and help with stormwater management and erosion control.

Green trees in summer and color-laden ones in fall are quintessential Vermont. There are nearly 825 million live trees in Vermont, making it the fourth most forested state in the United States. So it is not surprising that tree preservation and forest growth are top conservation priorities.

The highest national honor for any tree-friendly city is to be included on the Arbor Day Foundation's list of Tree Cities USA. Seven Vermont cities make that list, with Rutland the longest running, on the list for twenty-seven years. Other area Tree Cities with list longevity are Burlington, Montpelier, and South Burlington. Shelburne and Essex Junction are fledgling tree towns, and Middlebury was just added this year.

My guess is that Williston, Vermont, might be next, if you go by the number of new trees popping up around my son's home. Trees, the hope of our future . . . the cutting edge of green.

AUTUMN LEAVES

I WASN'T YET FINISHED SAVORING SUMMER THIS YEAR WHEN AUTUMN arrived. As usual, fall snuck up on me, jumped out, and shouted, "Boo!" Reality has an annoying way of intruding on our daydreams. Reverie is brief and so is summer in Vermont.

I was still floating on a cloud, adrift above the daffodils, still walking through the lush green of early evening dew, when suddenly fall rushed in. More than any other season, it seems autumn is the season of change, the time of passing.

Spring is about renewal, the return of warmth, life's reawakening. Summer is just plain fat and lazy here, and Old Man Winter, white and crusty. But autumn, when it comes, stomps its foot and demands our attention with its cacophony of color and parsimony of light. In October, daylight dwindles and the mountains dapple into pied beauty as autumn rings out a clarion call of change, giving us no choice but to listen.

I remember the signs of autumn growing up in suburban Philadelphia—brown wings that fell like miniature helicopters from oak trees and horse chestnuts breaking out of spiky green shells—both prized items for a child's treasure-trove collection. In high school, fall was the time to run the hockey fields and caravan through town on a Saturday afternoon celebrating a football victory.

Over the years I've learned the man-made signs of autumn in Vermont. Woodpiles climbing in driveways, ski racks back on top of station wagons, and newscasters telling us which parts of the state's foliage are "peak." I've lived through so many Vermont autumns now that I think I'm beginning to channel Robert Frost. Even his name speaks what lies just around the corner from autumn—frosty nights followed by the first early snow.

Fall is official now; that happens on the calendar with the autumn equinox. But there are more telling signs. The air that began to crisp a few weeks ago and the chill that started sneaking up on September nights tell me summer is past. Change is not only in the air, but in the light as the sun's arc shifts in the afternoon sky and stretches shadows long on the sidewalk.

Still, I think it's important in this raucous season to hold on to a moment in time. I don't want to count how many autumn leaves I've seen in my life or wonder how many autumns are left. I just want to savor the fading scent of hydrangeas when I walk to my door. I want to stand in the yard and look and listen to the squawking geese flying in V-formation high overhead. I want to linger on my afternoon walk, breathe in the crisp air, and study the shifting patterns of the shadows.

A season is passing, and I want to honor its presence in this moment, because another one exactly like it will never come again.

GOOD DAY SUNSHINE

"THE WEATHER OUTSIDE IS FRIGHTFUL," OR SO GOES THE HOLIDAY refrain. I think it might be better to say, "I can't see what the weather is like outside, because it's so gloomy and overcast." Dark December is, after all, a Vermont liability. That's one reason we delight in snow: It sparkles the landscape and brightens our spirits.

I think it's actually good cosmic planning to have the holidays stretch from late November through the end of December. Not only does this provide psychic energy and social chatter to sustain us during the sun's stingiest arc, but spending time in shopping malls provides welcoming light. It doesn't matter that it's artificial; it's light.

Sunshine, John Denver used to sing, "always makes me happy" and there's actually scientific evidence that sunshine—light—strongly affects our well-being. When a low-pressure system moves in, the sun moves out, producing a powerful drag on our mood as well as a pain in our knees and joints.

Winston Churchill, who often suffered bouts of depression, said, "Sunshine is my quest . . ." That same quest—to brighten our outlook as well as our day—is shared by millions afflicted with seasonal affective disorder (SAD). I keep my 10,000 lux light box right next to my computer and turn it on first thing in the morning before I even open up email.

We humans aren't the only ones in search of light, either. A cat curls with contentment in the warmth of a sunbeam. A sunflower turns its face toward the light. Metaphorically as well as physically, the sun is the center of our universe. Light brightens our day, illumines our lives, lifts our spirits.

I think my holiday of choice at this time of the year is December 21, when we celebrate the first day of winter. The shortest day of the year is also the day light returns, when sunshine begins to smile on us just a bit longer and the days begin to stretch, marching toward summer.

There's a blog that lists the top one hundred songs celebrating sunlight in their title. Right near the top are several songs by the cultural gurus the Beatles, who celebrate in harmony the wonder of sunshine. In her two-and-a-half-year-old wisdom, my granddaughter intuitively connects with their message and their music.

When I last visited her, we began each morning by climbing on the couch and opening the computer to listen to the Beatle classic, "Good Day Sunshine." Together we welcomed the day crooning, "I need to laugh, and when the sun is out, I've got something I can laugh about. I feel good in a special way. I'm in love and it's a sunny day."

The Beatles, music, and sharing the morning with my granddaughter—that beats a light box any day as the way to light up my life.

LORD OF THE MANOR

It's vacation time again for my friends of the many acre gardens, and I've been left in charge. The blueberries are bursting, and there's kale and chard in abundance. I've just picked the first corn of the season, and the summer squash and zucchini are a feast in yellow and green. Above it all preside the sunflowers, golden and majestic; and the sweet scent of phlox fills the air. Midsummer magic at the many acre farm.

When I'm finished for the evening, I share the back deck with Shady, my friends' farm dog. Together, we look out over the fields toward Mount Mansfield and the Greens, which rise and slope on the horizon. It feels good to share the evening with the land—and the dog. There's something very special about looking off into the distance and not into your next-door neighbor's kitchen.

For several years before we moved to Vermont, our family owned seven acres of meadow and woodland in rural Maryland. On weekends we'd flee the overcrowding of Washington, DC, and escape to our fantasy land abutting the Potomac River. We'd explore overgrown paths and pick wild berries. From a rise on the land, you could sit and watch turkey vultures glide in effortless flight. The air smelled fresh, and you could see for miles.

When we first moved to Vermont, our Shelburne house was on the edge of wooded land that was the frontier of exploration for our eight-year-old twin sons and Petie, their beagle buddy. As they grew older, weekends and summer vacations took the boys farther afield—backpacking on the Long Trail or camping—only at primitive sites, of course. But it was always about the lure of nature and exploration.

As a city kid from Philadelphia, I remember how excited I was to visit my grandparents' summer cottage in rural upstate Pennsylvania. There, water gushed from a pump, not a faucet, and the neighbors' cows would sometimes stroll up to the windows of the dining room. The bathroom was an outhouse down the path from the cottage. And afternoon excitement for us kids was gathering rocks to dam up a small field stream so we could swim in knee-deep water. The cottage sat on a dirt road that seemed to go nowhere, but for us it led to a truly a magic kingdom.

I realize that my happiest memories are tied to open land, the freedom of the uninhabited, where the only entertainment is the serenade of bullfrogs and the monotonous song of cicadas. Safely away from city streets, I treasure the solace of country living.

I still love museums, theaters, restaurants, and the night life of the city—but what truly feeds me is the land; and right now, as I tend my friends' gardens, I feed both body and soul.

I'm really beginning to cherish my friends' vacations—a time when I can partake of their bounty, walk the realm with Shady, and pretend I am lord of the manor.

PLANTING JUNE

My tomato plants got off to an early start this year, and now they're climbing high on the growth chart, boasting a profusion of yellow blossoms—looking just great. A gentlewoman farmer friend of mine in Warren—which is better known for snowbanks than early vegetable harvests—says her cabbage and kale are sprouting and the green beans have broken ground.

After the frigid winter we've just been through, there's nothing more satisfying than to glory in the lush green of our mountainsides and revel in the rich texture of just-plowed fields. We will of course have to wait until late August and the county fairs to see just how big the cucumbers and pumpkins grow this year, but they're off to a fructuous start.

One of the ways I survive the long weeks of winter is to imagine fall's cornucopia of vegetables. Another is to populate my living room with leafy plants. They're good company, but they seem to spend the months of winter drifting in the doldrums.

Then again, so do I. And in good bear tradition I also grow an extra layer of fat to insulate me against the long cold. Come summer I shed that winter accumulation by walking and weeding, finding ways to stay active. Summer's the North Country's reward for surviving six months of ice.

In winter, plants patiently endure limited light. But as the summer days stretch in length, plants reach heavenward. Blossoms laugh in riot, blooms love a crowd, beaches fill with children, bikers follow their path, creemee stands lift their shutters, and soon farmers will bring their bounty to market.

Tending houseplants through the winter teaches me patience and perseverance. Watching the explosion of my garden in summer fills me with hope and the wonder of anticipation. The greening of Vermont is underway.

June leaps off the calendar. It's a month of birth and rebirth as we celebrate the summer solstice, the day of summer's blossoming, the first day of the season that starts with hope and hopefully ends in abundance.

SAVORING NOTHING

I HAVE A FAVORITE BOOK ON MY "REREAD EVERY FEW YEARS" LIST. THE book is called *Zero: The Biography of a Dangerous Idea* by Charles Seife. It sits on my bookshelf next to a small volume entitled *Nothing: A Very Short Introduction* by Frank Close, a physics professor at Oxford University.

I have long been fascinated by the notion of nothingness. It's an enigma, a conundrum that has intrigued and bedeviled philosophers, theologians, and scientists from antiquity to Einstein. The Greeks in particular seemed to have had a fear of empty space, so they tried to rationalize away emptiness. Plato argued that by definition you can't have "nothing," and Aristotle concluded that emptiness doesn't exist, because "Nature abhors a vacuum." Over the ages the debate, the riddle, has continued to perplex thinkers, spawn theories, and raise more questions than answers.

It's hard to wrap your mind around nothing. It's hard to imagine the vastness of emptiness, to conceptualize "nothing," which is "something" that you can't see, feel, hear, or smell. Being in nothing isn't easy either, just ask someone who is learning to meditate. Lately, however, I'm becoming more comfortable with nothingness. After years overflowing with busyness, I enjoy those special moments of nothing but being— those moments when "nothing" happens and "nothing" is important.

On a recent sun-washed afternoon, I sat by the Burlington waterfront taking in nothing. It was the day an enervating heat wave finally broke, and under a crystalline blue sky the temperature was balmy and the humidity felt like, well, nothing. It was an exquisite day, one I wished I could bottle and label "Open in case of emergency after prolonged weather fatigue."

While I sat basking in my perception of nothingness, mesmerized by the shimmering sunlight on the waves and the lazy transit of billowed white sails across the lake, my young friend sitting with me looked at the scene and offered a different perspective. When summer comes to Vermont, he said, he can't find any of his friends. They're all out—busy hiking or boating, barbecuing and swimming, everyone doing something, Their "what-to-do-fun list" is full, and they are intent on not letting any of the fleeting summer season escape their grasp.

But while my young friend admitted he shared his peers' action imperative, he said he also wished for more alone time, more emptiness in his schedule. The generational divide wasn't as deep as I imagined. Together we sat by the lake at the end of a fishing pier, enjoying the expansive emptiness of the least-populated lake in the country and the silent ripple of mountain lapping beyond mountain far across the lake. Together we savored that special moment of doing nothing—which is, after all, everything.

SEASON WRAP

IN PLAIN SIGHT

I LOVE WATCHING THE RADIO. IT ILLUMINES SIGHT SO MUCH BETTER than television. Maybe it's because sound and stories stimulate my imagination and conjure vivid pictures in my mind's eye . . . or maybe it's just because I grew up in an audio age.

I don't think any HD screen can compete with the creaking doors or chilling music—the quaking quotient—of some of those vintage radio shows. What could be scarier than the menacing presence of *The Shadow* or the sound of the wind howling across the Yukon tundra as Sergeant Preston came on air.

What I like most about radio is what is missing. Instead of being told what to see, we must draw for ourselves a mental picture and color it inside our minds. We have to see the unseen and listen for innuendo— the frown or furtive glance, the moon casting a shadow, or an expression of delight at an aha moment.

Whether it was an edge-of-your-seat suspense show, the mystery of *Dragnet*, the soap opera *Romance of Helen Trent*, or the banter of George and Gracie, radio created a world that even today scares or excites in memory, a distant time rich in images, still loud in recall.

When I was a young teenager, one of the special moments was the Saturday afternoon broadcast of the local Philadelphia Phillies baseball games—the sounds, the mind's eye sights far richer and more evocative than any TV version of the game could ever be.

My guide for nine innings and three mesmerizing hours was Harry Kalas, the iconic play-by-play broadcaster known as the voice of the Philadelphia Phillies. Kalas beamed into the room his enthusiasm for the home team, and his words conjured magic. His signature tune when the Phillies won a game was, "High hopes, high apple pie in the sky . . . hopes." No sentiment better captures that fantasy called baseball. Kalas's legacy was that excitement for the home team. Forget the moving pictures on a screen. No one has ever visualized more dramatically that curving arc of a long fly ball heading toward the stands in left field: "Could it be . . . could it be . . . it . . . is . . . OUTTA HERE!"

Granted, without a video screen it's hard to tell who really is on first and instant replay is a game of blindman's bluff. Yet the pictures that the words created sear memory. Like the *Phantom of the Opera,* in order to see what is in plain sight, we must abandon our defenses—"Open up your mind, let your fantasies unwind."

In a way that TV cannot, radio stimulates our inner vision. It is the power of storytelling, words creating worlds. So, switch on the radio and tune in to the world through your mind's eye. It's all there in plain sight; we just have to open our imagination to see it.

HOPE SPRINGS ETERNAL

MARCH IS SANDWICHED BETWEEN OLD MAN WINTER AND CAPRI-
cious April. It's my month of hope, the month I've been waiting for since
last October, the month leading up to a new season when all things are
possible.

For me, the hope of March centers on that date circled in red on
my calendar announcing the opening of baseball spring training camp.
I know March is supposed to belong to basketball, the frenzy of March
Madness, with pools and brackets, Cinderella teams and the Final Four.

After all, I'm from Philadelphia, home of Villanova and Temple and
St. Joe's; I know my college basketball. I know that one of the greatest
Cinderella teams of all time was 1985 'Nova. But did you know the team's
legendary coach, Rollie Massimino, played three years of college basketball at the University of Vermont?

So this month I filled in my brackets and entered my friends' pools;
but my heart, my hope, lies 1,300 miles and twelve states due south—
down in Florida, with Peter Pan's band of boys. Down there, where right
now boys in men's bodies are swinging wooden sticks and throwing
cowhide balls, jockeying for position in the starting lineup and sliding
headfirst into the dirt.

Of course, I'm a Phillies fan. You can't be from Philadelphia and not
be a Phillies fan, just like you can't not like cheesesteak or Amish shoofly
pie. That would be akin to saying you're from Vermont and don't care for
maple syrup.

I know, of course, that Vermont is contiguous to Massachusetts and
the hometown team is the Red Sox. Actually, the two teams have a lot in
common—as in a lot of time between pennants—a lot more games lost

84

than won. And fans of both teams have a lot in common, too: a lot of passion, a lot of heartache—and a lot of this cockeyed thing called hope.

To be a Phillies fan—or a Red Sox fan—you have to just keep on believing. You have to be able to tell yourself, deep in September's cellar, that spring begins with a clean slate. And, actually, that's just the point. What other sport has as its moniker, "You gotta believe," and for its battle cry, "Wait 'til next season"? That's one of the beauties of this sport for me—its eternal optimism.

Every spring, right about now, as we anticipate the opening day of a new season, hope once again springs eternal for us long-suffering but faithful fans. Maybe this is our year . . .

Let's go Phils! (or Sox!) And will the last fan out the door on the way to the ballpark please take me?!

"SHOCK AND AWESOME"

In 2010, the United States was in economic freefall. It was the year of the Great Recession—and the era of Corporate Greed. Stories of personal hardship battled for headline space with accounts of bloated corporate and executive fortunes. It was a battle that greed seemed to win.

I guess that's why my pick for the "Best News Story of the Year" in 2010 was a sports story. *Time* magazine chose the creator of Facebook as their "Person of the Year," but I think the real hero was a baseball player.

Cliff Lee, the pitcher from Arkansas, provided the shock and awe story as 2010 drew to a close. Lee was considered the best pitcher in baseball at the time. But what he did that year said more about who he was, and his actions managed to bolster the spirit of a tired nation.

What he did, said one sports pundit, was "the unimaginable, the improbable, the unforeseeable." He walked away from a $30 million contract to chase a Little League dream of one day wearing a World Series ring. When money comes up against the intangible, it's usually money that wins. But not this time.

Lee jolted the sports world when he left his New York heiress at the altar and eloped with a charwoman from down the road. At the eleventh hour, Lee walked away from the vaunted, velvet Yankee pinstripes to sign with the blue-collar Philadelphia Phillies. A thirty-million-dollar walk to the City of Brotherly Love.

It seems Cliff Lee actually preferred scruffy Broad Street to the blinding lights of Broadway. Or as he put it, "At a certain point, enough is enough." *Enough is enough*—now, that's my pick for the 2010 "Yogi Berra Quote of the Year." Yogi couldn't have said it better.

It turns out that the Lee family all really *like* Philadelphia. Sir Cliff said the city is comfortable, a good fit for him—that he'd rather play with a team he respects in a city he loves. Or, as his wife explained, the family feels at home in Philadelphia, the food is good and so are the roads . . .

The New York Yankees offered Lee a longer contract with more money, and the Texas Rangers, the closest team to his home state of Arkansas, tried tugging at his roots. But the truth is, Cliff Lee had one more brass ring he wanted to grab, something just out of reach that he wanted more than anything . . . a World Series ring. Lee had been on the losing side of the last two World Series, and it looked like the Phillies gave him the best chance of grabbing that elusive prize.

Some things are worth more than money. You can't put a price tag on a dream, and you can't buy a World Series championship. Cliff Lee's dream was a victory ring—a World Series gold one. You gotta have a dream, said Bloody Mary in the show *South Pacific*. A dream is something that fills your soul in a way that dollars in your pocket never can.

In the end, it didn't work out for Cliff Lee. He and the Phillies never won the World Series. But during a very greedy time in our country, he reminded us that even thirty million isn't a number that adds up to happiness. As one of the 2010 sports page "pen-dits" put it: "Cliff Lee took less money and came up with the novel idea that Greed Isn't Good. Shock and awesome baby!"

FEASTING ON SUMMER

THE MID-JULY ALL-STAR GAME BASEBALL BREAK IS, FOR ME, THE OFFI-cial midpoint of summer in Vermont. And, as usual, I haven't had my fill.

I haven't been to the Burlington waterfront . . . enough. I haven't walked wooded paths enough or waded enough into the ripples of surf at Sand Bar State Park. I haven't gone up to St. J to see the stars or driven down Route 22A through the lush valley farmland.

What I haven't done is far more than what I have done—and, oh yes, the All-Star Game is just around the corner. I can feel the crisp, cold breath of autumn on my neck—and I don't want it to sneak up on me yet. I still have a lot of Vermont summer living to do.

Vermont is this amazing three-season tableau. The white comforter of winter settles down on the mountains and tucks in the towns. The crimson and fire of fall ignite the roadsides in an explosion of color. And where else is there a more radiant vision of summer than Vermont gussied up in her gown of emerald green?

I tell my siblings, remind my faraway sons, "Come. Visit. Indulge." But too often I also take for granted the unique treasure that is Vermont. I look beyond for more—the lights of Broadway, the museums of Wash-ington, the cafés of Montreal.

Yet, it is here in our backyard, in my backyard, in my Vermont, that I truly find my soul's nourishment. If I look up to the mountains or across the expanse of open lake, if I just look around—I know that here in Ver-mont is the green, green grass of my home.

Even though the calendar is dwindling down the days of summer, and the All-Stars are thinking about the homestretch swing through August's end, there's a lot of Vermont summer left to savor.

The banquet is still spread before me. In the weeks to come, I will swirl Vermont on my tongue and take a deep drink of reverie. On mild summer evenings, I will nudge myself down to the waterfront. On weekends, I will tear up my list of home projects and head out in search of dusty roads, local vineyards, and meandering streams.

I will remind myself that, in this fleeting moment we call summer in Vermont, the wild berries are ripe and waiting. I will rejoice in the land, along with an Irish poet-priest—Gerard Manley Hopkins—who wrote more than a century ago about his green native place. I will give thanks, as he did, for "dappled things," for "skies of couple-colour, brinded cows, trout that swim, and finches' wings" . . . I will say with him about my Vermont home, "Glory be."

SEASON WRAP

My team, the Philadelphia Phillies, won't be in the World Series this year. Instead, they'll finish the season with the worst record in baseball. Losing, it seems, is something my team does more often than winning.

Still, I care. Still, I sit by the computer every night during the summer, listening as the local Phillies radio commentary streams through cyberspace. I knew even before the season started that it was going to be a wash for my team—not like those glory days a few years back when the Phillies were serious contenders.

This is something Boston fans understand. One year the Sox win it all, take the pennant, and the next they sit alone in the division cellar. Ahh, the vagaries of baseball.

We carry our childhood with us all our lives. And at least for me, my childhood allegiance to a hometown baseball team is one of my fondest memories. I only ever attended a handful of Phillies games when I was young. But I still remember sitting in peanut heaven—the upper-level outfield cheap seats—for a doubleheader on a summer Saturday afternoon. It really was heaven for me, a lower-middle-class kid with a passion for baseball.

Baseball carries me through the seasons—there's the hope of spring when my team really could go all the way. Then come the hot, lazy days of summer when the slow-paced game seems just right for a sizzling afternoon—while in my heart, I still believe my team might have a chance to make it to the playoffs.

But as summer slips away in late September and we rush into autumn, so do my team's chances to make it into the postseason. The dreams and high hopes of many baseball teams wither with the chill of autumn, and if you're a Phillies fan, it's an all-too-familiar disappointment.

But autumn has its own refrain: *There's always next year.* That's one of the beauties of baseball—a game in which hope really does spring eternal. So, while the lucky few watch their teams vie for a spot in postseason festivities, I'll be thinking of greatness gone by ... and the month of April next, when baseball season starts again, when all things seem possible, and just maybe it will be the year of the Phillies—or the local hometown favorites, the Red Sox!

Play ball!

SHARED SPACE

SHARED SPACE

It wasn't exactly *The Brady Bunch*, but I grew up in a house with a brother, three sisters, two parents, a cat, and one bathroom—shared living before it had a name. It was the late 1950s, and sharing was a way of life. We shared toys and bedrooms; you took your turn on the phone and lined up in the morning for a spot at the bathroom sink.

Time to yourself was a precious commodity. Households weren't yet automated; food was cooked from scratch and carryout pizza hadn't been invented yet. There wasn't much time for daydreaming or a quiet space to write, at least for this young teenager who longed to be a writer. Maybe that was why I yearned for what Virginia Woolf called a "room of one's own," to have the resources and freedom to create.

In fact, a writing room of my own was a long time coming. The first was in the basement when I moved with my own young family to Vermont. Later, my space expanded to an entire unshared condo. I've lived alone for twenty years now, and though there are empty rooms, I write in an alcove of my living room. It is bathed in the extravagant warmth and light of the southern sun flooding through French doors—which is probably the closest I'll get to sitting and writing in a Left Bank café.

Ironically though, after years of writing alone, I've discovered one can have too much of a "room of one's own." That, while space, both physical and psychological, are essential to the creative process, just as important are connection and exchange, dialogue and support. Poets and writers have gathered to discuss their work since Chaucer's time in public houses, cafés, and empty rooms.

Hemingway in Paris didn't just write alone, he was part of a literary community that included Ezra Pound, Scott Fitzgerald, and Gertrude

Stein. In Key West, Hemingway labored in his writing studio, but he also held court at Sloppy Joe's, his favorite local watering hole.

Although it may not be Paris of the 1920s or Key West, Vermont is a writers' mecca. North to south, writers gather in neighborhood libraries and bookstores, in cafés and meetup groups to share their work and spur inspiration.

My hometown of Burlington is a burgeoning writers' community. Every week I can choose to join a poetry group or attend a memoir or creative nonfiction discussion. I'm able to interact with fellow writers as we thoughtfully critique each other's work, encourage each other's aspirations, talk about our craft and our vision. We share as peers and as mentors; in the process we become friends.

The hard work of creation must still be done alone, but thanks to the Burlington writing community, my room has expanded. I no longer feel so solitary, and because I can share, my work and my life are richer.

FOLLOWING A MICROCHIP

WHAT AN INCREDIBLE PLEASURE TO DRIVE THROUGH VERMONT IN THE winter, in the snow, with the sunlight smiling over the mountains. Driving deep through valleys, then driving high, breaking through clouds to touch the sky. No traffic, just the hum of snow tires on dry road.

I'm on a trip through Vermont, returning from Connecticut. A trip following a twenty-first-century star, my new friend and guide, my GPS navigation device. On the road again and headed home, my wagon hitched to a dashboard microchip.

I love the stand of stately birches, now bare, that hugs the guardrail as you enter I-89 near White River Junction, and the miles and miles of roadside conifers standing at attention. There are times along the way when the hillside slopes and you're at treetop level, sharing the view from above one minute and looking up at towering green the next. Trees majestic in a winter wonderland . . . mesmerizing. It's a good thing there's no traffic.

It's been a long time since I drove the interstate through Vermont. To me, it's one of the state's most scenic drives. There's so much of Vermont that is characterized by less. Less traffic, fewer people, no billboards. And right now, on the road, less is more. I was just over the state line near Brattleboro when I saw the first green license plate and a Holstein-patterned bumper sticker asking, "Got milk?" I knew I was home.

As much as I hate to admit it, this trip would never have gotten past dream stage if it hadn't been for my trusty GPS companion. I suffer from directional dyslexia; my personal genome profile has no map genes. The floating compass arrow in my head points north when I'm really headed west, and my internal MapQuest screams for a left turn when anyone else would know to take a right. I'm not very good at following instructions either, so this expedition with a bossy three-by-five-inch flat screen was a test of wills as well as of faith.

One of the characters in Harry Potter's *Chamber of Secrets* warns, "Never trust anything that can think for itself if you can't see where it keeps its brain." Well, I think my little GPS lady has all the potential for running amok like HAL in *2001: A Space Odyssey*. And like HAL, her simulated voice is smooth and seductive, telling me where to go if only I listen, if only I obey.

I am forced to take a deep breath and put my trust, my car, and myself in the control of a tiny but strong-willed microchip. North of Randolph the traffic begins to pick up, and, as always, I feel like I'm close to my Burlington home when I round that S curve above Montpelier and see the capital city nestled below.

My trip has been a success, and I grudgingly nod thanks to my GPS guide. But, like the henpecked Rumpole of the Bailey in the PBS series, under my breath I mutter, "She who must be obeyed."

DOGS AND LIFE LESSONS

I'VE NEVER BEEN MUCH OF A DOG PERSON, BUT MAYBE THAT'S CHANGING now, thanks to a couple of energetic, endearing canines with the classical names of Nero and Homer.

My son asked me to spend a week dog-sitting—or rather dog-walking—while he and his fiancé headed off to bask in the midwinter sunshine of Key West. I spent weeks in advance of the trip worrying about the challenges of an urban sojourn with two active dogs. I knew Nero, a five-year-old Australian shepherd, was well behaved, but I wasn't so sure about his younger brother. Homer is a barely one-year-old rescue dog of boundless energy and uncertain parentage, though probably part whippet and part herding dog. We're talking a challenge . . .

I admit I envisioned being pulled down the street by two racing dogs, me aloft in midair. But the reality proved far less intimidating than the anticipation. It didn't take long for Nero and Homer to win my affection, and the walks I feared became the highlight of my day. Nero with his regal gait and Homer, always on high squirrel alert, proudly introduced me to their neighborhood.

I understand now why dogs are more than just pets, they're members of the family. I have a son with two daughters, my granddaughters. And, thanks to his brother, I have two furry granddogs. The love for all is shared and genuine. Both my granddaughters and my granddogs have taught me about joy, about playing and sharing, about affection freely given and received, about jumping and dancing, about laughing and barking—that special canine expression of mirth.

My sister, who has fostered innumerable dogs over the years, says they are more loyal and nonjudgmental companions than humans. My friend, parent of Floyd, a floppy golden retriever, calls him the guru of joy.

"He lives totally in the moment," she says. "When I am with him, I realize how much I'm smiling, how happy he makes me feel. When we are out together walking in the woods, it's just fabulous. He feels, and he makes me feel, like isn't this just the best?"

I don't think I would have completely understood what my friend was talking about before I spent that special week bonding with my son's dogs and learning to love them—learning to appreciate the affection of a slurpy lick, to share the couch with furry creatures, and not tire of the endless games of "throw-the-toy-in-the-air-and-I'll-leap-up-and-catch-it."

I've come home now to my dogless Vermont condo. But still when I open the door, I half anticipate nuzzling dog greetings, and, to be honest, there are still mornings when I awake and wish there were two classical canines sitting next to my bed, looking up at me, and asking with their quizzical expressions, "When do we go for our walk?"

A SENSE OF PLACE

In the old song "Over the River and Through the Woods," we sing, "The horse knows the way to carry the sleigh" home for the holidays. But in the twenty-first century, it's easy to wonder, "Where is home?"

Home is an evasive place. Thomas Wolfe said you can't go home again; and someone else—maybe Bill Bryson—said you never really leave home, no matter how far you go. It challenges me to ask, "What does it mean, this 'sense of place'?"

Paris is my heart's home. It's the place of my imagination, the city that infuses my soul with dreams and hopes. It's the place I go to in memory and imagination when I am sinking into the doldrums of daily life. Paris is a real city I visit not nearly enough, and it's also a fantasy, a spirit I carry inside me.

Vermont is the place of my reality, the place I have called home for more than four decades. But to others not fortunate enough to live in this state of plenty, my reality is like a wistful dream, the place of their Norman Rockwell/Robert Frost imagination—a place they too would like to call home.

This Thanksgiving, for the first time in my long life, I will celebrate turkey and give thanks for family who live far away. No one will be coming home to Vermont, and I won't travel to be with my Philadelphia relatives. We'll spend the holiday apart, as life moves us all like pieces on a chessboard. So, this Thanksgiving will be a time for me to connect with friends rather than family, to be included in a twenty-first-century celebration that brings together neighbors rather than fathers and sons, aunts and cousins.

Today, I'll be traveling down the highway to Montpelier, welcomed by friends with open hearts and open arms. But I've also decided to open my home and my oven over the holiday weekend and welcome others who are living alone in this large neighborhood we call Greater Burlington. I make a mean apple pie, and there's nothing like next-day turkey gumbo.

The last Thursday in November is a time, as always, to give thanks for abundance—for food and friends, for love and family near and far away. It's also a time to reflect, to look around and see beyond ourselves, connect with someone who, like each of us, would welcome a smile, a handshake, a hug.

Perhaps in our peripatetic society, that's the new version of "Home is where the heart is"; that when we open our hearts, the geographic location of home keeps on growing.

I'll miss my sons and their families this Thanksgiving, as well as my siblings. My brother says the good news is he'll have more dessert without me there. I'll miss the traditional holiday stories passed between Mollie's green bean casserole and Keith's corn pudding, but I'll be hearing new stories shared at my friends' home. I'll also be collecting some new "old holiday traditions" from them, and I'll be creating some new ones for myself.

In fact, maybe this Thanksgiving, I'll really celebrate—and not come home until the cows do.

Happy Thanksgiving!

HOP ON A POEM

April, the month that honors poetry, opens with a nod to fools. Of course, poetry has nothing to do with fools—and everything to do with fools. Wise fools who speak in mime, who twist and play with words, who poke your consciousness and sear your heart. Poets stirring you to dream, encouraging you to wonder, to laugh and cry, to feel. Most of all, to feel.

Poetry expands our universe; it enriches our lives, because it speaks to the essence of being. The emotional life of poetry often begins with the seemingly mundane and leaps to the universal. It opens us to our sorrow and our hope. It takes us inside ourselves, telling us to slow down and be in this moment with ourself.

There are cerebral poets like T. S. Eliot and romantic ones like Wordsworth and Keats. There are poets who play with language like e e cummings, enigmatic poets like Emily Dickinson, and imagistic poets like the Russian Akhmatova. There are poets of place such as Carl Sandburg and beat poets, modern poets, and poets who write haiku. But whatever form poetry takes, it is universal and it is intensely personal.

I am a journeyman poet. I write to know myself, to give expression to what my heart is feeling, what my mind is thinking. When my soul's voice speaks its poetry, it may be as a sorrowful lament: "How quiet is snow at 4 a.m., how still the night . . ." Or it may be a glory song: "I feel wide and full of joy . . . I feel grass growing between my toes, I feel the changing wind . . ." What is important is that I allow it to speak.

It's encouraging that in our modern barren landscape of tweets and twitters, acronyms, and abbreviations, poetry is flourishing. The old-school fear of poetry has been replaced by an embrace of poetry's richness of expression. Poetry ignites the imagination of young and old. The young poet Amanda Gorman felt the pulse and captured the hearts of the nation when she recited her poem of hope at the recent Presidential Inauguration ceremony.

Across the board, studies show a quantum leap in adults and especially young people reading poetry. Some of the best writing in our local press can be found on the pages of the Young Writers Project here in Vermont. But poetry is an oral art, an auditory one, and the allure goes beyond just reading or writing. Throughout the country, in grade schools and high schools, spoken word and performance poetry events are increasing in popularity.

So then, how will you honor April, this tribute month of poetry? By choosing to ignore it in your life of more important things, or by finding a quiet corner in the midst of rush and run to renew an old friendship or begin a new one? It doesn't matter whether you prefer a sonnet to a haiku, or get lost in formless free verse. There are no poetry police to tell you what to like or not to like.

You chose to meander down a familiar lane with Robert Frost, rejoice with a poet priest in the glory of dappled things, or try your own hand in the expression of poetry. Whatever you choose, the opportunities are endless, the rewards priceless.

Happy April! Happy spring! Hop on a poem and go for a joyride!

THE GOOD NEWS

THE NEWS COMES IN VARIOUS SHAPES, SIZES, AND SHADES OF GRAY, SO I appreciate it when I find stories under the heading "Good News." Humanitarian stories that inspire and lift the bar instead of lowering it. That speak of kindness and remind us of our connectedness.

One such story appeared recently in the *Washington Post*, and I felt a personal connection.

After Hurricane Maria devastated Puerto Rico, there were many victims left behind and not all of them were human. Among the casualties were countless pets, some abandoned during the deluge, others lost in the ensuing chaos. To make matters worse, many pet shelters were swept away in the storm, leaving few resources.

Enter Lucky Dog Animal Rescue, a nonprofit organization in Arlington, Virginia, run by a network of dedicated volunteers and a dynamic director, Mirah Horowitz. Thanks to her commitment and resourcefulness, a planeload of dogs and cats was flown from San Juan, Puerto Rico, to Baltimore, Maryland.

The plane, donated by Southwest Airlines and operated by a volunteer crew, flew to San Juan with thousands of pounds of donated supplies (both people and pet varieties) and flew back with sixty-two abandoned canines in desperate need of new homes.

Lucky Dog has strict protocols for screening rescue dogs' health as well as the backgrounds of volunteers who foster the dogs and people seeking to adopt them. All the rescue dogs are medically examined and treated prior to being offered for adoption.

My son and daughter-in-law are "foster parents" with Lucky Dog Rescue, and through them, I've learned a lot about the rescue process and the transforming power of kindness in the lives of both people and pets.

Dogs arrive exhausted from the long journey, whether that journey has been by plane from Puerto Rico or on a long van ride from South Carolina. The dogs are often frightened or have been physically harmed by human abuse and neglect. Yet, little by little, the dogs become less fearful and withdrawn, more trusting. From foster volunteers like my son and his wife, they learn human kindness and affection. But perhaps even more important, from my son's two dogs they learn playfulness and acceptance.

The story of a planeload of rescued pets and my own experience watching my son's foster dogs have reminded me of the importance of compassion and caring. It's one of the stories that lifts the bar, a story that truly belongs under the heading "Good News."

FAR AND NEAR

ULYSSES MADE HIS ODYSSEY, GULLIVER HAD HIS TRAVELS, AND THE Canterbury lot headed off on a pilgrimage. Deep within us, it seems, there is wanderlust, that itch to see what lies beyond. To cross over the mountain, glide down the river, venture into the unknown—and then, of course, come home and tell stories about our adventures.

Early this fall I headed out on the trip of my dreams, following my curiosity across continents, traveling west to east physically and metaphorically, to cruise the Volga River through Russia, from St. Petersburg to Moscow.

Russia has always been my passion, my fascination. In my youth I fell in love with *Dr. Zhivago*. In college I shared the heart of *Anna Karenina* and delved the tortured conscience of Raskolnikov. I came to know *The Brothers Karamazov*, traveled the steppes in *War and Peace*, and followed the quietly flowing Don River. From Gogol to Chekov, from Tolstoy to Dostoevsky, from Pushkin to Akhmatova, I read thousands of pages, and I fell under the spell of Ruska. The vastness of its landscape, the tenacity and endurance of its people, its beauty and bleakness, the sense of mystery.

When I finally visited, the reality of Russia didn't disappoint, but it did surprise. I wasn't prepared for the breathtaking beauty of St. Petersburg and the lights and glitz of Moscow. St. Petersburg is known as the Venice of the North, and the Hermitage Museum, sitting on the banks of the Neva River, looms over the city like a cathedral, majestic with its blue façade and imposing statuary. Its grandeur is matched by the fountains and gardens of Peterhof, Russia's Versailles, and by Catherine the Great's summer palace, crowned with golden oval domes and lit from within by the mirrors and mosaics of the resplendent Amber Room.

From St. Petersburg I traveled eight hundred miles by riverboat to Moscow through seventeen locks. Along the way we stopped to admire a century-old church built without nails, experienced a local welcome during a visit in a Russian home, and wandered the streets of Burlington's sister city, Yaroslavl.

When we docked in Moscow, I was expecting to be greeted by a bleak and dour city, dominated by history, repression, and ghosts. Instead, I walked through the past and present in the streets Moscow and discovered a city of paradoxes.

The Kremlin Wall still looms, but there are also the stately painted spires of St. Basil's cathedral, the legendary Bolshoi Theater, and the sleek decorated interiors of the city's subway stations. With its abundance of cheap natural resources, Moscow lights up at night as you cruise the canals, and from the vantage point of Sparrows Hill, one looks out over a sprawling city.

Even though my visit was during a political lull in Russia, I was still haunted by the Soviet past. Having come of age in the 1950s and 1960s, my most daunting experience was standing at midnight on Red Square. There I was surrounded by silence, and by the deafening echoes in my mind of the Cold War. Time took me back as I stood in the square populated now by tourists, curious like me, where once there was the rumble of tanks and military parades.

I wasn't quite sure what to expect when I headed out on my journey; whether a lifetime of imagining this trip would be disappointing in reality. Russia is obviously too vast a land, a literature, and a history to understand in one short trip, but she opened her arms and welcomed me.

Perhaps the best way to know a country is to know its people. In Moscow I visited the home of a young Russian couple, Anton and Lena, who also crossed an ocean to visit a strange land. Several years ago they lived in Burlington, while Anton was a graduate student at the University of Vermont. This young Russian couple opened their hearts and home to me just as Vermonters had done for them. Wayfarers in a foreign land finding unexpected compatriots.

We sat in their kitchen and talked about Russia and Vermont, about first impressions, differences, and similarities. We each had made our odyssey, ventured into the unknown, and returned home with memories overflowing and stories to fill the night.

OLD FRIENDS

POSTMARKS

ONE OF MY FAVORITE HOLIDAY TRADITIONS IS IN THE MAIL—CARDS
from afar that fill my December mailbox with messages of now from
friends of then. Those special friends who form the time line of my life,
a card catalog of people who have touched me, often just briefly, but in
a special way. Special enough that we keep this holiday tradition alive,
renewing our ties each year, celebrating our successes, sharing our losses.

If life is a journey, then these are Chaucer's pilgrims, a richly diverse
collection of people who have shared my journey, each with a tale to tell.
Friends from college, old office mates, girlfriends, teachers—friends I
laughed with and cried with. Those who inspired me, those who grounded
me, the ones who lifted me up, who believed in me when I lost faith in
myself. Good friends, special people, each a part of who I am today.

There is something innate in us as human beings that compels us
to reach out and make connections. It is the reason we live in tribes, in
villages, surrounding ourselves with family and friends. It's what's behind
the casual but heartfelt admonition we speak in parting, urging each
other to "keep in touch." It's what Facebook in the twenty-first century
has built a fortune doing.

But in my un-Facebook existence, I keep in touch via postage
stamps, through Christmas-card connecting. Over the years, December
by December, I have seen my friends move through their professional
lives, marry (sometimes more than once), raise families, build homes,
travel to distant lands, and now, increasingly, retire and brag about their
grandchildren.

Most of my old friends I'll never see again, although each year we
write, "We really should try to get together this year . . ." A long time ago

Paul Simon sang about old friends. It was long before he himself was an old friend; he pondered from the vantage point of youth: "Can you imagine us years from today, old friends. Time it was and what a time it was . . . a time of innocence, a time of confidences."

That 1968 Simon and Garfunkel album was called *Bookends*. I guess what my friends and I have done is to make sure that on the shelf of our lives, between the bookends of then and now, are all our favorite volumes—the rare books, the first editions, the novel and poetic—the authors of our life story . . . *all the old friends* . . .

PASSAGES

A MONTH AGO I EMBARKED ON AN ADVENTURE TO SHARE THE BIRTH OF a new granddaughter and help smooth the transition for her two-and-a-half-year-old sister. But it turns out her sister didn't need much smoothing, she's already pretty good at transitions. That left me time to reflect on changes of my own.

I've always thought of this time of year, late in November, as a time of transition. A time when, reluctantly, leaves abandon the trees, birds join in a southern pilgrimage, green seeps to brown, and the sun slips into hiding.

It seems the transition of seasons feels even more poignant now, in this the autumn of my life, like time passing in slow motion. There was a time when my generation wore flowers in our hair, danced to the music in a muddy farm field called Woodstock, and carried placards as we marched through the streets, believing our passion could affect social change. The 1960s and 1970s defined us.

Now, in a new millennium, those numbers carry a different meaning. We, the generation who once believed no one over thirty could be trusted, are well into our sixties and seventies, often looking back more than we look forward.

It was midway through the 1970s that the writer Gail Sheehy gained fame chronicling life's transitions in her book *Passages*. She gave us a road map to help negotiate what she called the "Predictable Crises of Adult Life," the ones bubbling to the surface in our thirties, our forties and fifties.

She later followed up with a book updating her road map of passages, moving us through menopause, men's later life, and the life challenges of caregiving. Sheehy, now in her mid-seventies, forged her writing career telling us about transitioning to new stages of life.

In my mid-thirties, with the enthusiasm of youth, I wrote a book entitled *Successful Aging*. In it, I quoted Deane Davis, who served as Vermont's governor in the early 1970s. When Davis was in his early seventies, he used to tell the story of a man he knew who was so ready to die that he never bought green bananas.

"That's not the way to live," Davis admonished. "Go buy green bananas." In essence his message was to keep alive anticipation, to foster expectation. "Make sure," he said, "every day is full of life, full of adventure . . ."

I've noticed among my friends that accepting life's transitions helps them ease through the passage into later life and discover its unique rewards. Late in life, when we close the door on what has been, we open ourselves to what is in this moment. And that can bring not only satisfaction but deep joy.

Right now, for me, that's the immense joy of holding my newborn grandchild, or opening my arms to a goodnight hug from her sister, that little girl who lights my world when she smiles and says, "I love you, Grandma."

FRUITFUL SUMMER

THIS YEAR, MY SUMMER IS GOING TO BE A LITTLE LESS FRUITFUL—OR at least compared to recent years, it will be vegetable scarce. That's because my friends, longtime proprietors of what I call the many acre garden, are moving south. It's a combination of the allure of sunshine and the consequence of aging. My friends are craving warmth and relocating to a place where gardens don't grow in summer and snow doesn't fall in winter.

The title of this new chapter in their lives is "Retirement"; the backstory for me is saying good-bye. I guess like gardening, getting older is about seasons and change, about ripening and harvesting. About thinning and tending and uprooting.

Recently I've renewed an old friendship with the poet Emily Dickinson. She's good company in a sleepless night, sharing her musings on the ordinary and the extraordinary. In a poem I read a few nights ago, she speaks with eloquence of that special quality of light that comes in springtime, lingers briefly, and then is gone, a metaphor of both fullness and loss.

In my late-sixties life, it's not just the calendar that tells me I'm aging. My bones remind me every morning, my joints crackle, my stamina squawks. But life doesn't just take away. The beauty is in the paradox. As we age, we grow more forgetful and we remember more vividly. We feel contentment as well as regret. Our sleep patterns change, and we watch more sunrises. We slow down so we can catch up with our grandchildren, and we free ourselves of ambition and inhibition so we can remember how to play.

With my friends gone this summer, there will be less kale and fresh corn, less squash and fewer homemade berry pies. I'll miss barbeques on the deck, and, even more, I'll miss sitting with them and talking away lazy summer evenings.

But the good news, they remind me, is that their new Florida home is open for visitors and it's located just outside Clearwater, not far from Phillies Way. What a combination—Clearwater, spring training, my Phillies, and a place to stay . . . the future is good.

I think aging is a state of mind, and so is baseball. Baseball has always been my metaphor for hope. In the cold of January, it gives me something to anticipate; in the dark night of February, it shines with possibility.

Spring training opens during the blustery month of March, just as the sap is beginning to flow in Vermont and long before the cinder block plunges through the melting ice on Joe's Pond. Like that special light Emily Dickinson described, baseball arrives each spring, reminding us of what we value.

I love baseball, but I value friendship and family most, even if it means a lot more traveling to share them now. And as for that garden of plenty, maybe this summer I'll have to start planting my own.

NEW CITIZENS

This July Fourth an early-morning naturalization ceremony took place at Calvin Coolidge's birthplace in Plymouth. The setting was significant, because Coolidge was one of two presidents from Vermont and the only US president born on the Fourth of July. The swearing-in was both solemn and celebratory, with President Coolidge's great-granddaughter singing the national anthem.

Nineteen people stood that day and pledged their allegiance to the United States of America. Two of my neighbors were among them.

After forty years in the States, my Canadian neighbors in Shelburne have become citizens. They're the ones who regularly fly the American and Canadian flags on either side of their doorway and for years have hosted an annual neighborhood Fourth of July barbecue.

They're also the neighbors who snow-blow driveways up and down the street when a blizzard hits, host visiting international students, and lead Cub Scout and Brownie troops. Basically, they give meaning to the phrase "good neighbors."

But until a few weeks ago, they weren't American citizens. Their children were born here, and for more than thirty years they've called Vermont home. But for all these years my friends have been resident aliens. When I asked why they'd finally decided to become citizens of their adopted country, they said initially they wanted to wait until they could become American citizens without giving up their Canadian citizenship. Then somehow the years passed and they never followed up, until seven months ago when their green cards came up for renewal. Now, they decided, was time.

My neighbors returned home that day from the swearing-in ceremony, just in time to again host the midsummer Independence Day barbecue, that very American holiday. Two brand-new flags—one American and the other Canadian—unfurled in welcome by their front door. And from the neighborhood friends, there were clusters of balloons offering congratulations, as well as a tabletop picture slideshow of the morning's citizenship ceremony. But most proudly displayed were the framed certificates officially declaring my friends American citizens.

Of course, they'll always love deeply both the country of their birth and the country of their choosing. One of the privileges of American citizenship they say they'll cherish most is the right to vote, to voice their opinion and make it count on Election Day.

At the barbecue that afternoon, I stood on the deck listening to my friends talk enthusiastically about their new citizenship, and I felt proud for them. I also paused to consider how much I appreciate my *own* citizenship—that being an American is both a privilege and a responsibility. It is something we should never take for granted, something to be honored, not just on Independence Day but throughout the year.

VIRTUAL WINTER

THE SNOW LION OF MARCH CAME ROARING BACK TO VERMONT THIS past week, in a valiant effort to salvage our state's reputation as a white winter wonderland. But for my money, it's a case of too little, too late.

Vermont misplaced winter this year, buried it deep under the snow-drifts of late fall, and forgot to dig it out. Despite the recent tease of white crystals, green has been sprouting in my backyard, and winter mornings are filled with birdsong. I've already seen V flocks of Canada geese heading noisily north, and a few disoriented fruit trees in my neighborhood have started to bud.

In spite of the recent snowfall, this winter is likely to be one of the warmest and least snowy on record, a winter of endless balmy days, the year winter wasn't. And with climate change wreaking havoc with weather patterns, the future may be now.

This of course has challenged normally outdoorsy Vermonters to find snowless entertainment. We haven't been able to open the back door and glide away on cross-country skis. Snow blowers have pretty much been lonely hearts locked away in the garage; and, at least on Lake Champlain, much of the ice has been too thin for fishing shanties.

So, many Vermonters have turned to the alternate reality of life online. My friend Jane has been passing her evenings testing her wits playing Words with Friends, a cyberspace Scrabble game; while Tom, my politico friend, spends his time indoors with online debate. Others have satisfied their snow cravings in the cyber reality of Wii games, where you can virtually ski ravines and jump moguls in what seems to be real time.

But my friend Sally may have slipped furthest through the worm-hole into a parallel internet universe. She's fallen under the spell of eBay, seduced by the Lorelei of cyberspace bidding. It's become her mecca of choice; it offers more than enough diversion to fill long weeks of short days. She's been looking for the soft lavender birthstone of her dreams, and she's e-flipped her way through 727 online pages of amethyst rings, which is more variety than Ben & Jerry's has ice-cream flavors.

But despite the allure of the internet, I've pretty much decided that old friends are best for evening companionship. I don't own an e-reader like a Nook or a Kindle. I like holding a real book in my hands, reading poetry aloud, or listening to a Mahler symphony in stereo on the radio. I guess I prefer the proverbial slow lane, meandering like a brook or mulling life over a cup of warm cider.

And that, after all, is kind of like gliding on cross-country skis through the quiet of a moonlit snowy field—alone with the evening, following your own star, whether there's snow in the yard—or not.

WALKING PARTNER

MARY OLIVER IS GONE. I FEEL LIKE I'VE LOST A FRIEND, A SOUL MATE, A walking companion.

It was walks through nature that provided the inspiration for Mary Oliver's poetry. "For me the door to the woods," she said, "is the door to the temple." And it was in that temple that she worshipped—in silence, paying attention. Her "instructions for living a life," she said, were simple. "Pay attention. Be astonished. Tell about it."

It was in nature and solitude that Oliver found meaning and the life of her poetry. She spent nearly fifty years wandering the woods and coastline near her Provincetown home, pausing often to meditate and scribble. Nature spoke volumes to her, and she shared what she heard in twenty books of verse.

Although she won both a Pulitzer Prize and the National Book Award, what she really won was the hearts of people. Her goal was never critical acclaim, rather it was to share the life lessons she learned in nature.

Oliver paid close attention to details. She wrote about grasshoppers' "jaws" and the "skulls" of mushrooms. Always curious, she looked around her in awe of the natural world and was able to translate what she saw into words with healing power. It was words and nature, she acknowledged, that saved her own life. Growing up in a painful, abusive environment, Oliver later explained that what rescued her was "Poetry and the beauty of the world."

Mary Oliver wrote from her heart with accessible language about themes that mattered. Like many, I first became acquainted with her when a friend shared the poem "Wild Geese." "Whoever you are, no matter how lonely, the world . . . calls to you like the wild geese, harsh and exciting . . . announcing your place in the family of things." Those were words that resonated with me as a young woman struggling to find myself . . .

Later in life, I again found inspiration in an Oliver poem describing her day strolling through fields. She asks rhetorically in the poem, *The Summer Day*, "Tell me, what else should I have done?" Then she responds with a challenge that's become my own: "Tell me, what is it you plan to do with your one wild and precious life?"

Mary Oliver answered that question for herself in her late poem, "When Death Comes." The line she wrote is a fitting tribute to this extraordinary person, this iconic poet: "When it's over, I want to say, all my life I was a bride married to amazement."

RIPENING LIFE

THIS IS A YEAR OF MILESTONES IN MY LIFE, A YEAR OF DECADES. I'M IN my seventh decade now, and my daughter-in-law just entered her third. For my granddaughter, turning five years old, it's her first half decade. Milestones for us all, markers of miles, telling us how far we've come but not what lies ahead—which is what really tweaks my curiosity, wanting to know what lies around the next corner.

Irish poet Dylan Thomas, who died young from alcoholism, raged, "Do not go gentle into that good night," while British poet Robert Browning crooned, "Grow old along with me! The best is yet to be." But I like the backwoods Vermont wisdom of former governor Deane Davis best, when he advised friends to go out and buy green bananas to have something to look forward to.

I like the concept of waiting for life to ripen.

I have a friend who's always lamenting her physical limitations, focusing on what she can no longer do. I have to be careful or I find myself slipping into that same "can't do" frame of mind. The truth, of course, is that my joints don't move as well as they used to, and my bones often ache. My hearing isn't sharp, and my energy sags in late afternoon.

That's what I don't have.

What I do have is a full life with friends and family. I have grass, lush and green in my yard, and birds singing me awake on a summer morning. I have sun warmth that fills my living room and a canopy of stars smiling overhead at night. I have wonder . . .

As the poet T. S. Eliot put it, "I have books and cats . . . Life is good." I'll admit to having regrets in my life, but mostly I have rich memories. I have the stories of a lifetime, stories that make me laugh and ones that touch a sore spot in my heart. Stories full of the people and experiences that made me who I am today.

At seventy-plus, I also have perspective. What I value is in sharper focus. Not being so intent on achieving and on success, I can now appreciate smaller pleasures. What matters most are the values of compassion and understanding—how we treat each other and ourselves.

In this the year of decades, I'm aging backward, following the advice of Mark Twain: "Whatever [your] age, [you] can reduce it several years by putting a bright-colored flower in [your] button-hole."

I think that's a good formula for successful aging: a bright-colored flower, a smile, and a big bunch of green bananas.

PERSPECTIVES

QUESTIONING EINSTEIN

WE ARE ABOUT TO CELEBRATE ALBERT EINSTEIN'S 136TH BIRTHDAY, but who's counting? Einstein showed us, after all, that time and space are relative. He smashed like an atom our belief in absolutes. Nothing, he told us, except the speed of light is constant. Yet the irony is that he himself has become a timeless constellation in the universe of physics.

Einstein changed how we view the world. His theory of relativity is considered by many to be the biggest leap of the scientific imagination in history. In 1999 *Time* magazine named him "Man of the Century." And Einstein's influence, his work, is as significant today as it was more than a century ago when he told us that E=mc2—the equation that everyone knows, though relatively few understand.

Einstein is, in fact, a gift that keeps on giving. In a recently published article in the journal *Science*, researchers acknowledged that the massive explosions of four different supernovas they've been watching over the last decade are actually reruns of a single blowup.

Thanks to a phenomenon known as gravitational lensing, the scientists have been seeing the same nine-billion-year-old star exploding, but from different angles and different moments in time. Light rays from the exploding supernova were bent by the gravity of clusters of galaxies, putting them on a different path toward us. These four images grouped together make the shape of what is known as an Einstein cross.

Einstein would probably say it's all about how we look, what we think we see, and what is really there. "The true sign of intelligence," he said, "is not knowledge but imagination ... The important thing is not to stop questioning." Questions tweak our curiosity; they stir our complacency.

So, it seems fitting that to honor Einstein, his birthday has been designated International Question Day—a day when students worldwide are encouraged to question. For Einstein the thinker it wasn't about having all the answers, but opening yourself to not knowing. Being able to sit patiently in the limbo of the unknown. "I have no special talents," he once said, "I am only passionately curious."

Einstein was born in the Victorian Age of the nineteenth century. His work spanned the twentieth century, and his influence continues into the twenty-first, as a philosopher and educator as well as a scientist. Everyone, Einstein believed, is a genius, capable of great things.

What marks new advances, he said, is having the creative imagination to raise new questions and seek new possibilities. "Follow your curiosity," he urged, because "the most beautiful experience . . . is the mysterious."

Happy birthday, Albert.

I HAVE A DREAM

CIVIL RIGHTS LEADER MARTIN LUTHER KING JR. UNDERSTOOD THE power of words. He used them to motivate and inspire a generation. King's words never pandered, they never maligned or bullied. As a result, his eloquence still resounds, his lexicon of hope still inspires.

It has been more than sixty years since King dreamed a dream and told us about it. He stood in front of a statue, not a defiant Confederate leader, but the brooding figure of the Great Emancipator, Abraham Lincoln, and spoke about his vision for a great America. One that was compassionate and inclusive, a nation not diminished by bigotry and hatred, by racism.

More than 250,000 people filled the National Mall that August afternoon in 1963, anxious for the inspiration of a King. They weren't disappointed. Martin Luther King Jr. looked out over a sea of black and white faces, and the words he spoke became the clarion call of the Civil Rights movement.

"I have a dream today. . . " King said, "that my four little children will one day live in a nation where they will not be judged by the color of their skin but by the content of their character . . . I have a dream that one day this nation will . . . live out the true meaning of its creed . . . that all men are created equal."

But ironically, King's dream and its vision almost went unexpressed that day. For ten minutes King read from notes on the podium, his eyes cast downward. He talked about "a bad check, a promissory note that America defaulted on." Academic words, notes penned by an aide.

Then something quite amazing happened: A solitary voice spoke out. Standing behind King on the podium was gospel singer Mahalia Jackson, a longtime friend who sang just before he spoke. As King's speech lumbered on, Jackson knew something was wrong. Masked by a burst of applause, she cried out to King. . . "Tell them about the dream, Martin, tell them the dream . . ." King paused, set his notes aside, and, from his heart, began again . . .

"I say to you today, my friends, even though we face the difficulties of today and tomorrow, I still have a dream. I have a dream . . ."

The power and inspiration of that "I Have a Dream" speech is a cornerstone of our history and speaks to the hope of our future. We know King's dream because one woman had the courage to speak out, and because King on that August day in our nation's capital opened his heart and shared his dream of a truly great America.

HEARTSPUN HOPE

Even though the diminishing light of November and early December drags us into the doldrums, the holiday season arrives to lift us up just in the nick of time.

Thanksgiving and Christmas are back-to-back festivals. In late November we gather to give thanks, to celebrate abundance and family. Then comes December, when we step back in time, once again charmed by a belief in the red-suited Santa and reindeer that fly. That otherwise dark time of year that we light up with family and friends.

This year seemed even darker, as a divisive national election raged on with rancor and animosity. It tipped my mood toward despair, until I came across healing words from the mid-twentieth-century poet Carl Sandburg.

Somehow when long-winded exposition fails, poems in their brevity can speak volumes. They tell us what our heart already knows, if only we listen. At least that's how I felt when I stumbled upon Sandburg's poem "Hope Is a Tattered Flag."

The poem draws on Sandburg's deep understanding of the American character. It's part of his epic collection, *We the People, Yes*, written in 1936. Sandburg hoped his words in that dark time would rally the country mired in the throes of the Great Depression. Sandburg's three-hundred-page magnum opus was a tribute to the resilience of the American spirit, to the enduring power of hope. Hope, which Sandburg called "a tattered flag and a dream of time."

Sandburg reminds us that hope is always with us. It is present in the time of war as well as in peace. Because, no matter how deep our despair, "birds go on singing to their mates," spring grass "shows itself where least expected," and even in the "changeable sky" there is a "rolling fluff of white clouds."

Sandburg drew his inspiration from the Christmas season, that time of year when we are "buoyed . . . by children singing chorales . . . Bach being broadcast from Bethlehem, Pennsylvania . . . And the hands of strong men groping for handholds . . ."

For Carl Sandburg, the poet of the American spirit, hope is a "heartspun word." It is the light that breaks through our gloom and illuminates our way. But hope, he believed, is not just a healing force, it is also a provocateur. It is "the kiss, the comforting laugh and *(the) resolve*—"

So, this holiday season, I'll not only embrace hope, I will remember it is a two-edged sword. I'll let the poet's words help me reach beyond the rancor of politics and reclaim my hope, my belief in the strength of goodness and the power of kindness. I'll remember there is more that unites us than divides us. But I won't fall into complacency. I'll take up a personal gauntlet and commit myself to working for a better world during the holidays and beyond.

THE COST OF MEMORY

MEMORIALS COME IN ALL SHAPES AND SIZES. I HAVE A PIECE OF THE dismantled Berlin Wall. I have Civil War bullets from Gettysburg and Antietam. And I have, from my grandfather, a deep love of history and of country. I have a vial of volcanic ash a friend collected just weeks after Mount Saint Helens erupted. I have a brother who still carries his medals, his soul scars, from a year in the hell that was Vietnam.

Each of these memorials comes with the cost of memory.

Washington, DC, is the quintessential city of memorials. It glistens in late spring, an iridescent green presided over by the obelisk of the Washington Monument, and brooded over by a larger-than-life Abraham Lincoln. Just beyond is a wall of memory inscribed with the names of soldiers lost during the Vietnam era. And nearby, the soaring monoliths of tribute to the Greatest Generation, passing quickly now, but always to be remembered.

I remember those who lined the mossy green around the Reflecting Pool in front of the Lincoln statue to hear a Black preacher and icon of the Civil Rights era talk about his dream of equality. I remember marching in the streets of Washington; I remember watching riots in those streets, and I will always remember the sight of tanks and armed soldiers riding down Connecticut Avenue in the year of turmoil, 1968.

Most of all, though, the memorials I remember are the moments of silence and tears, of severed hearts and a crippled nation. I was just a cub reporter when I watched the funeral procession carrying the casket of Robert Kennedy drive beneath the grieving stare of President Lincoln. RFK, on his way to share his final resting place beneath the earth of

Arlington Cemetery. To lie next to his fallen brother, in the faint glow of an eternal flame.

By definition we do not erect memorials to victory. We build memorials to remember war's human cost or to honor statesmen who understand that blood was shed to preserve the liberties we hold self-evident. I have always been profoundly moved by the stark Wall honoring those who died in the Children's War that was Vietnam. But it is Franklin Roosevelt's memorial that, for me, resonates the most.

The words of FDR's weary condemnation of violence as the way to resolve conflict are etched in the granite walls of his monument. Words that speak in sad reflection what the Vietnam Memorial screams in emotion: "I have seen war," FDR said. "I have seen blood running from the wounded . . . I have seen cities destroyed . . . I have seen the agony . . . I hate war."

So many years later, so many memories more, as I reflect on Memorial Day, the day of remembrance, I too feel sadness and frustration. I wonder, *How long it will take for the lessons of the past to be learned? How long before conflict finds other means of resolution?*

I bow my head in tribute to those who have paid the ultimate cost. Lives lost or forever scarred. And I remember that every memorial comes with the cost of memory; I remember . . .

LEGEND AND LEGACY

WHAT A PRIVILEGE TO DELVE INTO THE HISTORY OF MY GENERATION through the cinematographic storytelling of Ken Burns on public television. One such odyssey chronicled the legend and legacy of two of my twentieth-century heroes, Franklin and Eleanor Roosevelt.

Although the Roosevelts, the Great Depression, and Second World War were more a part of my parents' generation, I've long been inspired by this courageous couple. By FDR's legacy of leadership and perseverance, of overcoming, and of hope—and by Eleanor Roosevelt's legacy of compassion and dogged commitment to human rights in all its forms.

Not long ago I made a pilgrimage to Hyde Park, New York, to visit Springwood, Val-kill, and Top Cottage—the physical and spiritual homes of Franklin and Eleanor Roosevelt. It was serendipity that my visit coincided with Burns's biopic on the Roosevelts, but it started me thinking about adversity and about overcoming.

Thinking about how some people who are afflicted with severe physical and emotional wounds are often able to reach deep within themselves and discover a wellspring of strength that enables them to achieve the seemingly impossible. And this gives them compassion toward others who face daunting challenges.

Eleanor Roosevelt has always been one of my heroes. Over the course of her public life, she shared a lot about facing adversity and overcoming it. "We gain strength, and courage, and confidence," the First Lady said, "by each experience in which we really stop to look fear in the face ... We must do," she admonished, "that which we think we cannot."

The FDR monument in Washington sits midway between the Jefferson and the Martin Luther King Jr. monuments. At the entrance is a bronze statue of Roosevelt sitting in his wheelchair. It's a glimpse of the president that few people outside his inner circle ever saw when he was president, a controversial image many objected to even including at his memorial.

Etched above the statue of the wheelchair are the words of his wife Eleanor: "Franklin's illness," the inscription reads, ". . . gave him strength and courage he had not had before. He had to think out the fundamentals of living and learn the greatest of all lessons—infinite patience and never-ending persistence."

I think Roosevelt's experience taught him more. I think through his own adversity he learned compassion for others whose struggles were often just as profound as his, and just as invisible. During the course of his presidency, FDR created programs that provided jobs and housing and food—the most fundamental of human needs—to millions ravaged by the nation's economic collapse. Just as important, Roosevelt restored dignity and offered hope to those mired in the devastation of the Great Depression.

That is, for me, the real legacy and the legend of FDR. The enduring legacy, the inspiring legend is how he struggled against adversity, how he persevered despite crippling challenges. And how, because of his own experience, he was able to give confidence and hope to others.

That same hope is what gets me through when my own days feel dark and daunting. That, and Eleanor Roosevelt's challenge to do, every day, "one thing that scares you."

WALLS OF RUIN

WALLS DOMINATED THE NEWS FOR YEARS AS A DEBATE RAGED OVER erecting a wall on our southern border with Mexico. The wall was meant to shut out the flow of immigrants, to "seal our safety."

The threatened wall galvanized public opinion and brought my attention to walls—their meaning and symbolism. Walls built to separate, built to keep others out and walls that seal us in. Physical walls and psychological walls.

Politicians and military leaders have a lot to say about walls, but so do poets. As a poet with a deep love of history, my interest in walls is both metaphorical and concrete. Walls stand as symbols of exclusion and threat, as well as protection and safety. It's a discussion that has intrigued thinkers over centuries, as they debate the value and fate of history's many walls.

In a poem written in the early 1900s, "A Fence—Poem," Carl Sandburg admitted that "a fence of iron bars with steel points" will effectively "shut off the rabble, vagabonds (and) hungry men," but, he added, that same fence will also shut out "all wandering children looking for a place to play." Sandburg concludes that though the fence may be a "masterpiece," its bitter mission is to allow nothing to pass . . . except "Death and the Rain and To-morrow."

The contemporary Native American poet Mien Bless also laments that walls and fences surround us everywhere, "creating boundaries both inside and out . . . " And she cautions, "It's about time we realize these walls and fences are just malice." Malice, built to divide, walls share the eventual fate of collapse.

My son and daughter-in-law spent a recent walking holiday along Hadrian's Wall in northeastern England. Constructed in the second century by Roman Emperor Hadrian, the wall stretches seventy-three miles from coast to coast, one of the most famous barrier walls in antiquity. In places along its route, the wall once rose twenty feet and sat as much as nine feet wide. Fortified by towers and defended by legions of Roman soldiers, it was a daunting symbol of military might.

But among historians, there's much debate as to the effectiveness of Hadrian's Wall. At least one scholar declared the wall represented an "ideology of empire"—a show of force that in the end was more message than effective deterrent.

Most of Hadrian's Wall now lies in ruin, many of its stones pilfered over centuries. Rather than a victory monument to exclusion, the wall has been transformed by time into a grassy hiking path overlooking pastures and rolling hills. Once mighty, Hadrian's Wall is today a crumbling reminder of the fleeting nature of power.

FATHER'S DAY THOUGHTS

With Father's Day just a couple days away, and Mother's Day only a few weeks gone, it's a time when most people take a moment to reflect on parental love and care.

But some of us had parents who were unable to provide the love and nurturing their children needed to grow and prosper—sometimes a parent fails his or her child.

And even if that failure isn't the kind of severe abuse or trauma that leaves debilitating wounds, it can still deeply impair a child's ability to thrive and develop. Although it may not be a case of malicious or intentional harm, parents sometimes just lack the crucial ability to provide love and connection. Stuck in reliving their own history, parents can pass on their own early pain and experience. But when the victim is a child struggling to thrive, intention doesn't matter.

For me, Father's Day and Mother's Day are not a time to praise my birth parents, but rather occasions to remember and acknowledge the unconventional parenting that helped me become who I am today.

In my life there were many unsung heroes who loom large. When I needed them, it was my extended family who stepped in. It was my grandfather and a slew of "greats"—great-aunts and great-uncles—who provided me with the nurturing I lacked at home.

Enter as well a long line of school teachers, sports coaches, and youth leaders who encouraged me and gave me a sense of value and self-worth. These were the special people in my childhood who offered me the gift of their unconditional love—caring people who may not have had any idea how transforming their gift would be.

I hold those healing memories close to my heart. I cherish these special people who gave me what my own parents could not—and it is their love that I acknowledge on these days of "remembrance."

But I know this story isn't mine alone.

So, this Father's Day, I invite others to join me in honoring anyone who's ever reached out and embraced a vulnerable child with wide open arms and a willing heart.

And I'll spend the day reflecting on love freely given to me by the many men and women whom I'm proud to call "my family."

STORIES IN THE NIGHT

EVERY CHILD NEEDS A HERO

MINE WAS GREAT AUNT VIRGIE—A HERO IN HIP WADERS; A LARGER-
than-life presence who stood barely five feet tall, wore an apron, and
knotted her hair in a bun. Someone who could make even a small child
feel important by the way she tilted her head toward you, listened ever so
carefully, and smiled readily with approval.

Her house sat high on a ridge overlooking an aging industrial city in
upstate Pennsylvania, but to me it sat in the heart of Never-Never Land.
Not as in never grow up, but as in never turn down a challenge, never give
up, and never, never let anyone say a girl isn't good enough.

In a time when women wore skirts and kept house, Aunt Virgie wore
waders to go trout fishing, bagged bear, and tracked deer. For us kids, visiting her house was going on safari. Stuffed deer trophies with fearsome
antlers crowded the walls, and a slightly ratty moose head tried to look
regal. On the bookcase a squirrel stood bolt upright; and sprawled on the
living room floor were a pair of very large, very black, and very scary bear
rugs, heads intact, mouths opened in roar.

All were trophies of time Aunt Virgie and Uncle Ira spent hunting
and fishing at their camp in Potter County, up north on the Pennsylva-
nia/New York border. Back then, Potter County, much like Vermont's
Northeast Kingdom, seemed to have more deer than people, more hunting camps than houses. Wildlife roamed the woodlands, and streams ran
with trout. It was a place of dreams and legend.

Although I didn't know it then, the Potter County camp was Aunt
Virgie's best gift to my sisters and me. In a time when horizons for girls
were limited, Aunt Virgie showed us something else by her example. She

gave us large footprints to step into and opened wide our sense of wonder. She challenged us to dream big and inspired us to go after our dreams.

About the time summer vacation drew to a close each year and we kids prepared to head home, early apples hung red and tempting on Aunt Virgie's front yard tree. "You can have the apples that have fallen to the ground," she would tell us, "or pick the ones that are easy to reach." But the best apples, the tastiest ones, she challenged us, "are the ones you need to climb high for. The ones that make you reach."

Aunt Virgie never wrote a book or inspired a movement. Her name can't be found on any list of famous women. But if we've been very fortunate, there's a woman—a mother, aunt, or teacher—who, like Great Aunt Virgie, touched our lives. Someone who shared their eyes so we could see the world in a different way. Who encouraged us, who listened. Someone seemingly small who was in fact much larger than life.

TREES AND TRADITIONS

My mother wasn't German, but her signature Christmas carol could have been "O Tannenbaum." Decorating the Christmas tree was one of her most treasured holiday traditions. A week before Christmas, with us kids in tow, my mother would walk the three blocks to our local elementary school tree lot where she would barter for the ideal tree—in her mind that could only be a perfectly conical, sweet-smelling Scotch pine. Then, with my sister hoisting the front end and me dragging the trunk, we kids would balance the tree in our wagon and head homeward in an evergreen Christmas parade.

Once we had the tree in the living room, the challenge of stabilizing it in its stand was a feat of civil engineering, while stringing the lights was a test of patience and wits. Half a century ago, the fat multicolored light bulbs could be unscrewed and rearranged—which my mother did obsessively, making sure no two identically colored bulbs ever nestled too closely together. The desired effect was a perfectly random look that was anything but.

Next came the hanging of the ornaments. The assorted ornament collection contained a time line of kids and school projects—the kindergarten Popsicle-stick sleds, the second-grade baked-dough candy canes, the pipe-cleaner stars, and the third-grade intricately painted stained-glass angels. We kids finally had our turn hanging the Christmas balls, but my mother was right behind us to rearrange any clashing color schemes.

Those trees of childhood still live in my mind's eye, monuments to my larger-than-life memory of Christmases past. Somehow it just doesn't seem like Christmas without a tree. Yet, here I am in mid-December . . . fir-less, pining, treeless.

I now celebrate Christmas Day in a distant city with my children and a grandchild, so having a real tree doesn't seem to make much sense. I light up the house in December with candles and decorate with vintage holiday ornaments. But I miss the center of attention—the tree. Life of course is simpler without a fresh-cut Christmas tree—nothing demanding to be watered, no cascading needles to be swept up, and no brittle branches to drag curbside in early January.

I know not having a Christmas tree is most sensible—but sensible really isn't what Christmas is about. To me Christmas is about childhood magic—a red-suited phantom, reindeer that fly, and a live tree spreading its branches, growing in the middle of the living room. So next year, even if I travel afar, I think I'll decorate a Christmas tree and let the sight and scent rekindle the warm glow of memory. Like my mother, I'll celebrate the joy of the season in pine and with the carolers recite the old refrain, "O Tannenbaum, O Tannenbaum, your branches green delights us."

VISION-ARY

"I CAN SEE CLEARLY NOW," JOHNNY NASH SANG BACK IN 1972, "THE RAIN is gone." For me, it's the clouds. I see clearly now thanks to state-of-the-art lens implants that have replaced my cataract-clouded ones. For too long I have been looking at life through a veil darkly; now I see images with high-def clarity in Blu-ray color. Light has new meaning, and my life has new vision.

Cataracts growing over the lens of my eyes turned my world milky. I looked out through the drape of a sheer curtain. I had forgotten how rich the hue of red can be, how blue the sky is, what white-white really looks like. Suddenly, with my new eyes, Vermont greens are greener, and this year's fall foliage is rioting with color.

I've long appreciated the painter Paul Gauguin's observation that "I close my eyes in order to see." Gauguin was talking about the power of seeing through the inner eye, that wonderful eye of imagination, so rich and evocative. But for me there is new excitement. I'm seeing clearly for the first time in forever what is really there.

I've actually had a hard time getting adjusted to seeing. It is only now that I can see sharply and clearly that I realize how impaired my vision has been. Sometimes we know something best because we have experienced its opposite; our awareness grows keener in the presence of absence. I know victory because I have tasted defeat. I love warmth because I have been cold. I fathom fullness because I have plumbed emptiness. And I appreciate my sight even more because I have experienced the world diminished.

Change for me this fall is not just about trees and leaves; the changing light is not just about days growing shorter and the transition to a new season. I joke with friends that I am growing a bionic body, new eyes and knees just a few years old, joints of titanium. I move more freely now; I see more clearly. I also question less often where the path I am taking will lead.

Even though I see more with my eyes open, like Gauguin I still need to close my eyes to get my bearings. I need to close my two eyes so that my third eye, that eye of imagination, my sexton, can show me my path.

It turns out it takes time and effort to see with clarity what is really there. It also takes practice to trust the vision of the third eye. So, in reality and in metaphor, it is as Johnny Nash sang way back then . . . "Gone are the dark clouds that had me blind, it's gonna be a bright, bright sunshiny day."

DISCOVERING NEW WORLDS

In our changing world of reality, what was once accepted is no more. Heroes we once took for granted are knocked from their pedestals, their statues are crashing down. That is the fate not just of Confederate generals but of school class heroes like Christopher Columbus. The fact is Columbus didn't "discover" America; he never even set foot in North America. More important, his legacy is tarnished by the reality that Columbus represented the onset of a painful history in the Americas, an era of brutal Spanish colonialism and exploitation.

To right the perspective, a number of states have changed the holiday designation of Columbus Day to Indigenous Peoples' Day in honor of the native people, the First People, who were the original inhabitants of the New World. What is important is not the celebration of a conqueror, but the spirit of exploration.

I like that concept, honoring the importance of discovery. It is the spirit of adventure that expands our inner world, as well as the world around us and the space beyond. As the astronaut Sally Ride said when she became the first woman in space, "There's something magical about pushing back the frontiers . . ."

Apparently, many early explorers got their inspiration reading *The Travels of Marco Polo*. For me, the lure and love of adventure came from reading the novels of Mark Twain, who wrote about adventure along the Mississippi. Twain's young hero, Huck Finn, floated down the river that at the time was almost as inhospitable as the turbulent ocean sailed by early explorers. But it is Twain's advice that has always spurred me on: "Sail away from the safe harbor," he said. "Catch the trade winds in your sails. Explore. Dream. Discover."

Sharing that spirit of discovery, I'm about to be off on an adventure myself. Off to celebrate the wonder of new life, the birth of my grand-child. I'll be transported on a south wind to Washington, DC, the place my son and his family now call home. I want to be on hand for the arrival of Granddaughter Number Two, to share the beginning of her great adventure.

My sons when they were little, and now my first granddaughter, have taught me that no one loves adventure more than a child. Children are our role models, off to explore the world as soon as they can crawl, find-ing endless adventure in the backyard grass or setting sail in an oversize cardboard box. Children look at the world through eyes of curiosity; they explore through touch and taste. Their imagination is limitless.

Eleanor Roosevelt once said, "I think, at a child's birth, if a mother could ask a fairy godmother to endow it with the most useful gift, that gift should be curiosity." There's certainly no end to my grandchild's curi-osity, to her sense of wonder. But there are all kinds of adventures, and they aren't solely the domain of the young.

I have a friend who's a doctor, and another who's a stone carver. I have a nephew who waits table so he can live his dream to be a singer, and I have a sea captain friend who spins tall tales, speaks bits and pieces of for-eign languages, and has never lost his wanderlust, his love of adventure.

And that's what I think we should be celebrating on this Discovery Day. Not the tarnished legacy of Columbus, but that spirit of adventure that propels us to sail uncharted waters, to gaze at the distant horizon and dream of what lies beyond. To experience the joy of lying in the grass with a child and looking into the sky for cloud fantasies. To sprinkle fairy dust along our path, eat ice cream from a runcible spoon, and look up into the night sky, laughing and cheering on that spotted Holstein who is trying to leap the moon in a single bound.

BLACK HOLES AND BUTTERFLIES

ACCORDING TO RECENT NEWS REPORTS, AN INTERNATIONAL TEAM OF physicists has discovered what they call the God particle, the singular, smallest substance responsible for all else, the spark that may have ignited the Big Bang, the secret that unlocks the secret to everything.

Ever since Eve chose to eat from the Tree of Knowledge rather than accept the bliss of obedience, we've been dissatisfied with the ephemeral. We want explanations, we want to know the reasons why, and our curiosity of mind is the story of civilization, our never-ending efforts to reach beyond, to understand.

"One small step for a man," Neil Armstrong said after walking through space to step onto the surface of the moon. "One small step for a man, one giant leap for mankind."

I must admit I have a fascination with space and with wonderful, imaginative words and concepts like *event horizon, parallel universe, worm hole*, and *dark matter*. I'm especially intrigued by black holes that turn on themselves, swallowing whole stars, then spitting out the energy to create new life. Just as the humus of the forest floor nurtures growth on Earth, so from the darkness and death of distant cannibalized stars comes the intense explosion of energy that eventually creates new stars and galaxies.

Perhaps most mind-boggling has been the "discovery" that we can't account for 95 percent of all matter. It's hiding out of reach, out of sight, out of touch, but we know it's there because *it has to be*—we need it to explain everything "else." Without dark matter and dark energy, nothing else makes sense.

I applaud these efforts to explain existence, I find them fascinating. But then I also marvel at the simple yet complex beauty of a rose, the smell of lavender, and the flight of a fragile-winged butterfly. I'm filled with wonder when I see the intricate beauty of a newborn baby's hands and the weathered face of age, full of the beauty of years, of experience, of living.

Maybe scientists are in fact close to explaining how it all started, how we got from there to here and perhaps even where everything is headed. In the meantime, I'm just going to fill my life with as much of the mystery of living as I can.

I'll fill my days with the awe of a pink and purple sunset over the lake, with the simple pleasure of strolling down a back-country road. I'll savor the joys of summer in Vermont, the smells and sights of the ordinary that make life special, the sounds of quiet, the heartbeat of contentment— the small steps that are for me just as important as the giant leap; I'll celebrate what lives around us and in us—without which we can't really understand all that looms beyond.

TELL ME WHAT YOU SEE

ONE OF THE MAGIC GIFTS OF CHRISTMAS IS TO SEE THE WORLD through a child's eyes. To stand in the glow of a fir tree and see the wonder of green. To believe a red-suited old man can actually shimmy down the chimney. Who but a child has the faith and vision to know that reindeer really can fly and snowmen can come to life? A child looks through the third eye of imagination and sees sugar plums dance, hears reindeer prancing on the rooftop.

Imagination is a particular gift of childhood. It's not something we can wrap up in a pretty package or bottle for later use. It's a gift to be accepted without question . . . a star to follow, a dream to dream. It's what the artist Paul Gauguin meant when he said, "I close my eyes in order to see."

My four-year-old granddaughter is a wizard of imagination. Magic enriches her life; it expands her world. Never bored, she can flit like a butterfly, leap like a frog, roar like a lioness, or purr like a kitten. She doesn't need expensive props to play doctor. She rushes a couch ambulance through traffic to take her little sister to the hospital, where she tips an imaginary glass of water to her sister's lips and orders porridge and bed rest for three-seventy days.

She can host an impromptu marshmallow roast in front of the gas fireplace or climb Jack's beanstalk in the living room. Imagining Christmas, she sees in her mind's eye a decorated Christmas tree touching the ceiling of her gingerbread house. She can smell the cookies her mother is baking even though her mother's at work, and watch snowflakes fall— even when it's fifty degrees outside and raining.

Like Gauguin, my granddaughter and I play a game of imagination. We close our eyes to see what we can see and, in the process, discover a rich and wonderful world where all things are possible, including the peace on Earth imagined by angels and wise men in the centuries-old Christmas story.

It's the beauty and power of imagination that fuels dreams like the one of equality Martin Luther King Jr. dreamed so many years ago, or the shared, peace-filled world Beatle John Lennon imagined. Those dreams may not yet have come true, but as Bloody Mary sang about Bali Hai in *South Pacific*, you need a dream in order for it to come true. Or as my granddaughter says, "Close your eyes, Grandma. Now tell me what you see."

STORIES IN THE NIGHT

I AM NOT KNOWN FOR MY WEALTH OF KNOWLEDGE ABOUT POP CULTURE. But I have discovered the Cliffs Notes of catch-up streaming on my laptop. I am now working my way through the music of my generation that somehow I missed. Catching up with Pink Floyd, the Jersey Boys, and the Who, and making magic with some old friends, all of us off in search of America.

When I tire of music, I can curl up with words. I frequently invite Maya Angelou over for tea, and she regales me with the lilt of her voice and the laughter in her eyes. Mary Oliver usually can't make tea; she's out walking the shoreline. She drops by in early morning instead, toting her binoculars on life and reassuring me I do not have to crawl a hundred miles through the desert, repenting.

If the poetry seems a little tame, I hop on a light beam and probe the mysteries of distant space. Last week a flash of light flirted with me on my fifteen-inch monitor, a kind of cosmic Match.com. Unfortunately, that star wink, a dimpled twinkle from the most distant object in the universe, occurred nearly fourteen billion years ago, not long after the Big Bang gave birth to the universe.

There's not much chance of a dancing date with that starlet.

It's been racing to meet me since the dawn of time, but it died trying, swallowed up by a black hole not long after it twinkled my way. In this modern fantasy of illusion, I am looking through the warp of time and space, watching live what is not there.

If I don't feel so adventurous, I can just settle back into recent time past and spin the kaleidoscope of my own history. Along with a crowd of a few hundred thousand, I can listen to a proud Black man standing in the shadow of Abraham Lincoln, telling me about his dream in the summer of 1963.

Then, clicking a link, I travel ahead forty-six years and listen to a Black woman sing with heart and soul about the bell ring of freedom, claiming the promise of Martin Luther King Jr.'s vision. That raw January morning so many years later, was the dawn of the new day King had dreamed of, the inauguration of America's first Black president.

Aretha Franklin, the woman in the winged victory hat singing that morning about liberty and freedom, was the same Lady of Soul who back in the 1960s taught me about Respect. It is a message, one of the songs of my generation, that I did not miss.

Such is the variety of my evenings, the spice of my life. I don't have a cat to talk to, or a parakeet who sings to me. But I do have a techno-friend to help me make it through the night. A twenty-first-century Scheherazade with enough stories to fill a thousand and one starry evenings.

About the Author

Vermont is **Anne Averyt**'s home and wellspring of inspiration for the past forty years. Averyt is best known for her magazine and press features and her on-air voice as a longtime contributor to the Commentary Series on Vermont Public Radio. She is also the author of two nonfiction books, a memoir, and a poetry chapbook, *Autumn's Yard*.

"Anne Averyt has written a love song to Vermont. She glories in the seasons and shares the delights of living in Vermont in a series of descriptive essays. Vermonters and tourists will find much to smile about here."
—Madeleine M. Kunin, former Vermont governor
and author of *Coming of Age: My Journey to the Eighties*

"Anne Averyt knows Vermont. Her short essays remind us that autumn here can be seen in the color of light as well as the color of leaves, and that any season is enhanced by a flavoring of literature. This is a book replete with deep memories and sharp insights, one worth dipping into anytime."
—Tom Slayton, former editor-in-chief of *Vermont Life* magazine

"Anne Averyt captures the spirit of Vermont in stories that are short on words, but rich in imagination."
—Jerry Greenfield, cofounder of Ben & Jerry's

"This is a wonderful collection of essays with a distinct sense of place. It transports the reader to particular moments in time that are familiar and rooted, and that savor our deep connections to nature."
—Robin Turnau, former president and CEO of Vermont Public Radio

"'Follow your curiosity,' Einstein urged. . . . And so Averyt does in this rich collection of essays that weave personal and universal connections with time, place, and context. Join Averyt's old friends and journeying pilgrims for history, humor, and a healthy appreciation of both human and mother nature."
—Sarah W. Bartlett, poet, essayist,
and founder/facilitator of *WomenWritingVT*